The
Rigging Math Made Simple
Workbook

Delbert L. Hall and Brian Sickels

Spring Knoll Press
Johnson City, Tennessee 37601

Table of Contents

Acknowledgements

We would like to thank Shane Martin and Dennis Booth for their assistance with proof reading this book. Also, a special thanks to Simon Captain Howdy for his help in finding and correcting errors after the original printing of the book.

Introduction

It is sometimes said by realtors that the three most important factors in starting a successful business are "location, location, and location." If this is true, then the three most important factors in learning a skill are "practice, practice, and practice." The purpose of this book is to help you practice your rigging math skills.

This work book is a companion to *Rigging Math Made Simple*, second edition. Each "Chapter" in this book corresponds to the "Lesson" with the same number in the other book. At the end of each Lesson in that book there were a few "Sample Problems" for you to solve. This book is a response to requests from riggers and educators for more problems and answers.

Each Chapter provides you with the equation(s) that you need to know to solve the problems in that chapter and an example. This example shows you how to solve the problem - all math or techniques included. Additional explanations appear in some chapters. The main part of each chapter are the problems for you to solve. The answers to the problems are given at the end of each chapter, or sometimes at the end of each section of a chapter.

If your answers are not <u>exactly</u> the same as ours, do not fret. Ask yourself, "How close do I need to be?" Of course, you want to be as accurate as possible, but rigging is not the same as precision machining, where your tolerance might be +- one ten-thousandth of an inch (0.0001). If you are calculating the load on a chain hoist, being within a few pounds is close enough. If you are calculating the length of a bridle leg, being within an inch is probably close enough.

If you are having difficulties, review the Lesson in *Rigging Math Made Simple*, second edition, to refresh you memory. You can also ask for help on or Facebook group https://www.facebook.com/groups/1383812178507795/

We hope this workbook is beneficial and "happy rigging."

- Delbert Hall and Brian Sickels

Unit I:

Conversions

Chapter 1:

Converting between Imperial and Metric Units

Converting Meters to Feet

$Meters \times 3.28 = Feet$

Example: 7 meters is equal to how many feet?

7 meters × 3.28 = 22.96 feet

Problems

1. 87.4 meters is equal to how many feet?

2. 193 meters is equal to how many feet?

3. 1,013 meters is equal to how many feet?

4. 458.4 meters is equal to how many feet?

5. 0.45 meters is equal to how many feet?

6. 8.32 meters is equal to how many feet?

7. 349.2 meters is equal to how many feet?

8. -45.3 meters is equal to how many feet?

9. 1,244 meters is equal to how many feet?

10. 0.377 meters is equal to how many feet?

11. -4,398 meters is equal to how many feet?

12. 0.0045 meters is equal to how many feet?

13. 34.43 meters is equal to how many feet?

14. 996 meters is equal to how many feet?

15. 434.5 meters is equal to how many feet?

16. 66.53 meters is equal to how many feet?

17. 42,165 meters is equal to how many feet?

18. 56.3 meters is equal to how many feet?

19. 9.59 meters is equal to how many feet?

20. 1,953 meters is equal to how many feet?

Answers

1. 286.672 feet	8. -148.58 feet	15. 1,425.15 feet
2. 633.04 feet	9. 4,080.31 feet	16. 218.218 feet
3. 3,322.64 feet	10. 1.23655 feet	17. 138,301 feet
4. 1,503.55 feet	11. -14,425 feet	18. 184.664 feet
5. 1.476 feet	12. 0.01475 feet	19. 31.4551 feet
6. 27.2896 feet	13. 112.93 feet	20. 6,405.83 feet
7. 1,145.37 feet	14. 3,266.87 feet	

Converting Feet to Meters

Feet / 3.28 = Meters

Example: 30 feet are equal to how many meters?

30 feet / 3.28 = 9.146 meters

Problems

1. 324 feet is equal to how many meters?

2. 222 feet is equal to how many meters?

3. 0.543 feet is equal to how many meters?

4. 488.5 feet is equal to how many meters?

5. 4 feet is equal to how many meters?

6. 34 feet is equal to how many meters?

7. -56 feet is equal to how many meters?

8. 348 feet is equal to how many meters?

9. 98 feet is equal to how many meters?

10. 220 feet is equal to how many meters?

11. 590 feet is equal to how many meters?

12. 23.1 feet is equal to how many meters?

13. 55.3 feet is equal to how many meters?

14. 2.14 feet is equal to how many meters?

15. 11.4 feet is equal to how many meters?

16. -34.4 feet is equal to how many meters?

17. 88.63 feet is equal to how many meters?

18. 101 feet is equal to how many meters?

19. 444 feet is equal to how many meters?

20. 1,000 feet is equal to how many meters?

Answers

1. 98.7804 meters

2. 67.6829 meters

3. 0.16554 meters

4. 148.932 meters

5. 1.21951 meters

6. 10.3658 meters

7. -17.073 meters

8. 106.097 meters

9. 29.878 meters

10. 67.0731 meters

11. 179.878 meters

12. 7.04268 meters

13. 16.8597 meters

14. 0.65243 meters

15. 3.4756 meters

16. -10.487 meters

17. 27.0213 meters

18. 30.7926 meters

19. 135.365 meters

20. 304.878 meters

Converting Centimeters to Inches

Centimeters $\times 0.3937 = Inches$

Example: 20 centimeters are equal to how many inches?

20 centimeters 0.3937 = 7.874 inches

Problems

1. 38 centimeters is equal to how many inches?

2. 838.3 centimeters is equal to how many inches?

3. 43 centimeters is equal to how many inches?

4. 64 centimeters is equal to how many inches?

5. 483.2 centimeters is equal to how many inches?

6. -32 centimeters is equal to how many inches?

7. 24.3 centimeters is equal to how many inches?

8. 3 centimeters is equal to how many inches?

9. 77 centimeters is equal to how many inches?

10. 8.8 centimeters is equal to how many inches?

11. 0.43 centimeters is equal to how many inches?

12. 945 centimeters is equal to how many inches?

13. 57 centimeters is equal to how many inches?

14. 73.4 centimeters is equal to how many inches?

15. 49 centimeters is equal to how many inches?

16. 62.2 centimeters is equal to how many inches?

17. 45.3 centimeters is equal to how many inches?

18. 81 centimeters is equal to how many inches?

19. 292 centimeters is equal to how many inches?

20. 68.9 centimeters is equal to how many inches?

Answers

1. 14.9606 inches
2. 330.038 inches
3. 16.9291 inches
4. 25.1968 inches
5. 190.235 inches
6. -12.598 inches
7. 9.56691 inches

8. 1.1811 inches
9. 30.3148 inches
10. 3.46456 inches
11. 0.16929 inches
12. 372.046 inches
13. 22.4409 inches
14. 28.8975 inches

15. 19.2913 inches
16. 24.4881 inches
17. 17.8346 inches
18. 31.8897 inches
19. 114.96 inches
20. 27.1259 inches

Converting Inches to Centimeters

Inches / 0.3937 = Centimeters

Example: 7 Inches are equal to how many centimeters?

7 inches / 0.3937 = 17.78 centimeters

Problems

1. 87.4 inches is equal to how many centimeters?
2. 44 inches is equal to how many centimeters?
3. 465 inches is equal to how many centimeters?
4. -32 inches is equal to how many centimeters?
5. 0.0998 inches is equal to how many centimeters?
6. 46.34 inches is equal to how many centimeters?
7. 33.95 inches is equal to how many centimeters?
8. 4,392 inches is equal to how many centimeters?
9. 0.4998 inches is equal to how many centimeters?
10. 2 inches is equal to how many centimeters?
11. 10 inches is equal to how many centimeters?
12. 100 inches is equal to how many centimeters?

13. 1 inch is equal to how many centimeters?

14. 43.2 inches is equal to how many centimeters?

15. 765 inches is equal to how many centimeters?

16. 64 inches is equal to how many centimeters?

17. -0.654 inches is equal to how many centimeters?

18. 72 inches is equal to how many centimeters?

19. 48 inches is equal to how many centimeters?

20. 25.89 inches is equal to how many centimeters?

Answers

1. 221.996 cm	8. 11,155.7 cm	15. 1,943.1 cm
2. 111.76 cm	9. 1.26949 cm	16. 162.56 cm
3. 1,181.1 cm	10. 5.08 cm	17. -1.6611 cm
4. -81.280 cm	11. 25.4 cm	18. 182.88 cm
5. 0.25349 cm	12. 254 cm	19. 121.92 cm
6. 117.703 cm	13. 2.54 cm	20. 65.76 cm
7. 86.2331 cm	14. 109.728 cm	

Converting Millimeters to Inches

$Millimeters \times 0.03937 = Inches$

Example: 25 mm are equal to how many inches?

25 mm $\times$ 0.03937 = 0.98425 inches

Problems

1. 87.4 millimeters is equal to how many inches?

2. 193 millimeters is equal to how many inches?

3. 1,013 millimeters is equal to how many inches?

4. 458.4 millimeters is equal to how many inches?

5. 0.45 millimeters is equal to how many inches?

6. 8.32 millimeters is equal to how many inches?

7. 349.2 millimeters is equal to how many inches?

8. -45.3 millimeters is equal to how many inches?

9. 1,244 millimeters is equal to how many inches?

10. 0.377 millimeters is equal to how many inches?

11. -4,398 millimeters is equal to how many inches?

12. 0.0045 millimeters is equal to how many inches?

13. -34.4 millimeters is equal to how many inches?

14. 99.6 millimeters is equal to how many inches?

15. 434.5 millimeters is equal to how many inches?

16. 66.53 millimeters is equal to how many inches?

17. 421.6 millimeters is equal to how many inches?

18. 56.3 millimeters is equal to how many inches?

19. 9.59 millimeters is equal to how many inches?

20. 1,953 millimeters is equal to how many inches?

Answers

1. 3.440938 inches

2. 7.59841 inches

3. 39.8818 inches

4. 18.0472 inches

5. 0.01771 inches

6. 0.32755 inches

7. 13.7480 inches

8. -1.7834 inches

9. 48.9762 inches

10. 0.01484 inches

11. -173.14 inches

12. 0.00017 inches

13. -1.3543 inches

14. 3.92125 inches

15. 17.1062 inches

16. 2.61928 inches

17. 16.5983 inches

18. 2.21653 inches

19. 0.37755 inches

20. 76.8896 inches

Converting Inches to Millimeters

Inches / 0.03937 = Millimeters

Example: 0.45 Inches are equal to how many millimeters?

0.45 inches / 0.03937 = 11.43 mm

Problems

1. 64 inches is equal to how many millimeters?

2. 44 inches is equal to how many millimeters?

3. 96 inches is equal to how many millimeters?

4. 34.2 inches is equal to how many millimeters?

5. 1 inch is equal to how many millimeters?

6. 10 inches is equal to how many millimeters?

7. 25 inches is equal to how many millimeters?

8. 54 inches is equal to how many millimeters?

9. 23.55 inches is equal to how many millimeters?

10. -345 inches is equal to how many millimeters?

11. 0.8367 inches is equal to how many millimeters?

12. 77.4 inches is equal to how many millimeters?

13. 243.2 inches is equal to how many millimeters?

14. 0.1023 inches is equal to how many millimeters?

15. 887 inches is equal to how many millimeters?

16. 100 inches is equal to how many millimeters?

17. 333 inches is equal to how many millimeters?

18. 49 inches is equal to how many millimeters?

19. 81 inches is equal to how many millimeters?

20. 50 inches is equal to how many millimeters?

Answers

1. 1,625.60 mm
2. 1,117.60 mm
3. 2,438.40 mm
4. 868.681 mm
5. 25.4000 mm
6. 254.000 mm
7. 635.001 mm

8. 1,371.60 mm
9. 598.171 mm
10. -8,763.0 mm
11. 21.2522 mm
12. 1,965.96 mm
13. 6,177.29 mm
14. 2.59842 mm

15. 2,2529.8 mm
16. 2,540.00 mm
17. 8,458.21 mm
18. 1,244.60 mm
19. 2,057.40 mm
20. 1,270.00 mm

Converting KiloNewtons to Pounds

$$KiloNewtons \times 224.8 = Pounds$$

Example: 25 kiloNewtons are equals to how many pounds?

$$25 \, kN \times 224.8 = 5,620 \; pounds$$

Problems

1. 22 kiloNewtons are equal to how many pounds?
2. 32.4 kiloNewtons are equal to how many pounds?
3. 18 kiloNewtons are equal to how many pounds?
4. 12.44 kiloNewtons are equal to how many pounds?
5. 324 kiloNewtons are equal to how many pounds?
6. 3 kiloNewtons are equal to how many pounds?
7. 10 kiloNewtons are equal to how many pounds?
8. 1 kiloNewtons are equal to how many pounds?
9. 100 kiloNewtons are equal to how many pounds?
10. 88 kiloNewtons are equal to how many pounds?
11. 77.3 kiloNewtons are equal to how many pounds?
12. 36.32 kiloNewtons are equal to how many pounds?

13. 93.2 kiloNewtons are equal to how many pounds?

14. 0.43 kiloNewtons are equal to how many pounds?

15. 5.3 kiloNewtons are equal to how many pounds?

16. 0.36 kiloNewtons are equal to how many pounds?

17. 65 kiloNewtons are equal to how many pounds?

18. 54 kiloNewtons are equal to how many pounds?

19. 78 kiloNewtons are equal to how many pounds?

20. 25.2 kiloNewtons are equal to how many pounds?

Answers

1. 4,945.6 pounds

2. 7,283.52 pounds

3. 4,046.4 pounds

4. 2,796.51 pounds

5. 72,835.2 pounds

6. 674.4 pounds

7. 2,248 pounds

8. 224.8 pounds

9. 22,480 pounds

10. 19,782.4 pounds

11. 17,377 pounds

12. 8,164.73 pounds

13. 20,951.3 pounds

14. 96.664 pounds

15. 1,191.44 pounds

16. 80.928 pounds

17. 14,612 pounds

18. 12,139.2 pounds

19. 17,534.4 pounds

20. 5,664.96 pounds

Converting Pounds to KiloNewtons

Pounds / 224.8 = kiloNewtons

Example: 1,500 pounds is equal to how many kiloNewtons?

1,500 pounds / 225 = 6.6667 kN

Problems

1. 5,000 pounds is equal to how many kiloNewtons?

2. 1 pound is equal to how many kiloNewtons?

3. 100 pounds is equal to how many kiloNewtons?

4. 43 pounds is equal to how many kiloNewtons?

5. 56.9 pounds is equal to how many kiloNewtons?

6. 887 pounds is equal to how many kiloNewtons?

7. 23.54 pounds is equal to how many kiloNewtons?

8. 2,398 pounds is equal to how many kiloNewtons?

9. 8,453.4 pounds is equal to how many kiloNewtons?

10. 4,532 pounds is equal to how many kiloNewtons?

11. 8,883 pounds is equal to how many kiloNewtons?

12. 3,323 pounds is equal to how many kiloNewtons?

13. 1,109 pounds is equal to how many kiloNewtons?

14. 8,347 pounds is equal to how many kiloNewtons?

15. 434.5 pounds is equal to how many kiloNewtons?

16. 66.53 pounds is equal to how many kiloNewtons?

17. 42,165 pounds is equal to how many kiloNewtons?

18. 564.3 pounds is equal to how many kiloNewtons?

19. 91.59 pounds is equal to how many kiloNewtons?

20. 1,953 pounds is equal to how many kiloNewtons?

Answers

1. 22.2419 kN

2. 0.00444 kN

3. 0.44483 kN

4. 0.19128 kN

5. 0.25311 kN

6. 3.94572 kN

7. 0.10471 kN

8. 10.6672 kN

9. 37.6023 kN

10. 20.1601 kN

11. 39.5151 kN

12. 14.782 kN

13. 4.93327 kN

14. 37.1307 kN

15. 1.93282 kN

16. 0.29595 kN

17. 187.566 kN

18. 2.51023 kN

19. 0.40742 kN

20. 8.68772 kN

Converting Kilograms to Pounds

Kilograms $\times$ 2.2 = Pounds

Example: 8 kilos are equals to how many pounds?

8 kilograms $\times$ 2.2 = 140.8 pounds

Problems

1. 88 kilos are equals to how many pounds?

2. 45 kilos are equals to how many pounds?

3. 10 kilos are equals to how many pounds?

4. 2,455 kilos are equals to how many pounds?

5. 432 kilos are equals to how many pounds?

6. 0.934 kilos are equals to how many pounds?

7. 83,492 kilos are equals to how many pounds?

8. 145.3 kilos are equals to how many pounds?

9. 1,244 kilos are equals to how many pounds?

10. 0.377 kilos are equals to how many pounds?

11. 9,785 kilos are equals to how many pounds?

12. 0.0045 kilos are equals to how many pounds?

13. 34.43 kilos are equals to how many pounds?

14. 996 kilos are equals to how many pounds?

15. 23 kilos are equals to how many pounds?

16. 69 kilos are equals to how many pounds?

17. 57.34 kilos are equals to how many pounds?

18. 56.3 kilos are equals to how many pounds?

19. 9.59 kilos are equals to how many pounds?

20. 1,959 kilos are equals to how many pounds?

Answers

1. 193.6 pounds	8. 319.66 pounds	15. 50.6 pounds
2. 99 pounds	9. 2,736.8 pounds	16. 151.8 pounds
3. 22 pounds	10. 0.8294 pounds	17. 126.148 pounds
4. 5,401 pounds	11. 2,1527 pounds	18. 123.86 pounds
5. 950.4 pounds	12. 0.0099 pounds	19. 21.098 pounds
6. 2.0548 pounds	13. 75.746 pounds	20. 4,309.8 pounds
7. 183,682.4 pounds	14. 2,191.2 pounds	

Converting Pounds to Kilograms

Pounds / 2.2 = Kilograms

Example: 3,000 pounds is equal to how many kilograms?

3,000 pounds / 2.2 = 136.3636 kilograms

Problems

1. 10 pounds is equal to how many kilograms?

2. 100 pounds is equal to how many kilograms?

3. 60 pounds is equal to how many kilograms?

4. 45.3 pounds is equal to how many kilograms?

5. 398 pounds is equal to how many kilograms?

6. 9,823 pounds is equal to how many kilograms?

7. 722.4 pounds is equal to how many kilograms?

8. 7,548 pounds is equal to how many kilograms?

9. 475.3 pounds is equal to how many kilograms?

10. 33 pounds is equal to how many kilograms?

11. 98 pounds is equal to how many kilograms?

12. 34.3 pounds is equal to how many kilograms?

13. 0.435 pounds is equal to how many kilograms?

14. 0.0093 pounds is equal to how many kilograms?

15. 344.2 pounds is equal to how many kilograms?

16. 783.9 pounds is equal to how many kilograms?

17. 123 pounds is equal to how many kilograms?

18. 987 pounds is equal to how many kilograms?

19. 1,994 pounds is equal to how many kilograms?

20. 1,990 pounds is equal to how many kilograms?

Answers

1. 4.54545 kg	8. 3,430.9 kg	15. 156.454 kg
2. 45.4545 kg	9. 216.045 kg	16. 356.318 kg
3. 27.2727 kg	10. 15 kg	17. 55.909 kg
4. 20.5909 kg	11. 44.5454 kg	18. 448.636 kg
5. 180.909 kg	12. 15.5909 kg	19. 906.363 kg
6. 4,465 kg	13. 0.19772 kg	20. 904.545 kg
7. 328.363 kg	14. 0.00422 kg	

Unit II:

Pulley Math

Chapter 2:
Resultant Forces

Resultant Forces

This chapter covers calculating the resultant force on beams (or any point) that is attached to a pulley. To calculate this force you must know the inclusive angle of the line (fiber or wire rope) that is reeved around the pulley, and the load being lifted/supported by the line. You will need a scientific calculator to solve this type of problem.

The formula for calculating the resultant for is:

$$Resultant\ Force = Load \times \frac{sine\ of\ angle}{sine\ of\ (angle/2)}$$

Example: What is the resultant force on a beam supporting a pulley where the inclusive angle is 75 degrees, and load supported by the line is 350 pounds?

$$Resultant\ force = 350\ pounds \times \frac{sine\ of\ 75\ degrees}{sine\ of\ (75\ degrees/2)}$$

$$Resultant\ force = 350\ pounds \times \frac{sine\ of\ 75\ degrees}{sine\ of\ 37.5\ degrees}$$

$$Resultant\ force = 350\ pounds \times \frac{0.965925826}{0.608761429}$$

$$Resultant\ force = 350\ pounds \times 1.586706681$$

$$Resultant\ force = 555.347\ pounds$$

Resultant Force at Zero Degrees

When the angle of the line is zero degrees, such as with a block-and-tackle, use the following rules to find the resultant force on the beam:

- If the working end of the line is coming off of a <u>stationary</u> pulley, then

  Resultant Force = Load + force need to support the load

- If the working end of the line is coming off of a <u>moving</u> pulley, then

  Resultant Force = Load - force need to support the load

<u>Problems</u>

1. What is the resultant force on a beam when the load being lifted is 530 pounds and the angle of the cable is 64 degrees? $RF = 530 \times \frac{\sin 64}{\sin 32}$ $RF = 898.931 \text{ lbs}$

2. What is the resultant force on a beam when the load being lifted is 423 pounds and the angle of the cable is 120 degrees? $423 \times \frac{\sin 120}{\sin 60}$ $RF = 423 \text{ lbs}$

3. What is the resultant force on a beam when the load being lifted is 600 pounds and the angle of the cable is 34 degrees? $600 \times \frac{\sin 34}{\sin 17}$ $RF = 1,147.57 \text{ lbs}$

4. What is the resultant force on a beam when the load being lifted is 4,093 pounds and the angle of the cable is 153 degrees? $4,093 \times \frac{\sin 153}{\sin 76.5}$ $RF = 1,910.98 \text{ lbs}$

5. *Moving* What is the resultant force on a beam when the load being lifted is 500 pounds and the angle of the cable is <u>180 degrees</u>? $500 \times \frac{\sin 180}{\sin 90}$ ~~$RF = 500 \text{ lbs}$~~ $500 - 500 = 0 \text{ lbs}$

6. *Stationary* What is the resultant force on a beam when the load being lifted is 500 pounds and the angle of the cable is 0 degrees? $500 + 500 = 1,000 \text{ lbs}$
   ~~Moving or stationary pulley?~~

7. What is the resultant force on a beam when the load being lifted is 500 pounds and the angle of the cable is 90 degrees? $500 \times \frac{\sin 90}{\sin 45}$ $RF = 707.11 \text{ lbs}$

8. What is the resultant force on a beam when the load being lifted is 593 pounds and the angle of the cable is 36 degrees? $593 \times \frac{\sin 36}{\sin 18}$ $RF = 1,127.95 \text{ lbs}$

9. What is the resultant force on a beam when the load being lifted is 467 pounds and the angle of the cable is 67 degrees? $467 \times \frac{\sin 67}{\sin 33.5}$ $RF = 778.85 \text{ lbs}$

10. What is the resultant force on a beam when the load being lifted is 2,200 pounds and the angle of the cable is 75 degrees? $2,200 \times \frac{\sin 75}{\sin 37.5}$ $RF = 3,490.75 \text{ lbs}$

11. What is the resultant force on a beam when the load being lifted is 4,500 pounds and the angle of the cable is 26 degrees? $4,500 \times \frac{\sin 26}{\sin 13}$ RF = 8,769.33 lbs

12. What is the resultant force on a beam when the load being lifted is 342.5 pounds and the angle of the cable is 20 degrees? $342.5 \times \frac{\sin 20}{\sin 10}$ RF = 674.59 lbs

13. What is the resultant force on a beam when the load being lifted is 883.2 pounds and the angle of the cable is 166 degrees? $883.2 \times \frac{\sin 166}{\sin 83}$ RF = 215.27 lbs

14. What is the resultant force on a beam when the load being lifted is 300 pounds and the angle of the cable is 179 degrees? $300 \times \frac{\sin 179}{\sin 89.5}$ RF = 5.24 lbs

15. What is the resultant force on a beam when the load being lifted is 254.3 pounds and the angle of the cable is 60 degrees? $254.3 \times \frac{\sin 60}{\sin 30}$ RF = 440.46 lbs

16. What is the resultant force on a beam when the load being lifted is 2,359 pounds and the angle of the cable is 36 degrees? $2,359 \times \frac{\sin 36}{\sin 18}$ RF = 4,487.08 lbs

17. What is the resultant force on a beam when the load being lifted is 880 pounds and the angle of the cable is 55 degrees? $880 \times \frac{\sin 55}{\sin 27.5}$ RF = 1,561.14 lbs

18. What is the resultant force on a beam when the load being lifted is 444 pounds and the angle of the cable is 78 degrees? $444 \times \frac{\sin 78}{\sin 39}$ RF = 690.11 lbs

19. What is the resultant force on a beam when the load being lifted is 10,000 pounds and the angle of the cable is 12 degrees? $10,000 \times \frac{\sin 12}{\sin 6}$ RF = 19,890.44 lbs

20. What is the resultant force on a beam when the load being lifted is 310 pounds and the angle of the cable is 86 degrees? $310 \times \frac{\sin 86}{\sin 43}$ RF = 453.44 lbs

What is the resultant force on the beam supporting the following rigs?

21.

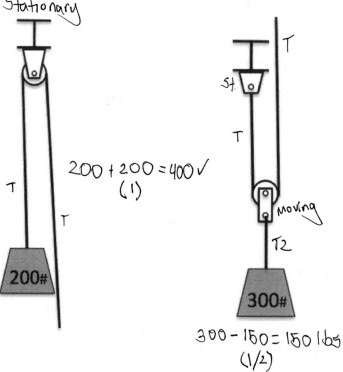

Stationary

$200 + 200 = 400 \checkmark$
(1)

T

T

T

200#

22.

T

St.

T

Moving

T2

300#

$300 - 150 = 150 \; lbs$
(1/2)

23.

2T

2T

Moving

T

3T

100#

T

$100 - 33 = 66 \; lbs$
(1/3)

24.

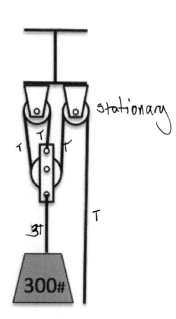

stationary

T   T   T

T

3T

T

300#

$300 + 100 = 400 \; lbs$
(1/3)

25.

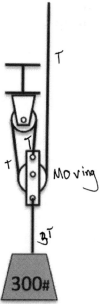

T

T

T

Moving

3T

300#

$300 - 100 = 200 \; lbs$
(1/3)

26.

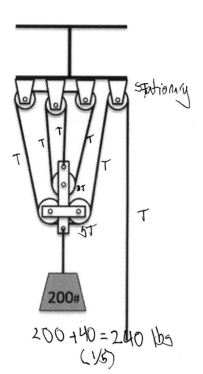

Stationary

T   T   T

T

T

3T

5T

T

200#

$200 + 40 = 240 \; lbs$
(1/5)

Answers

1. 898.93 pounds
2. 422.99 pounds
3. 1,147.56 pounds
4. 1,910.98 pounds
5. 0 pounds
6. 1,000 pounds
7. 707.1 pounds
8. 1,127.95 pounds
9. 778.85 pounds

10. 3,490.75 pounds
11. 8,769.33 pounds
12. 674.59 pounds
13. 215.26 pounds
14. 5.235 pounds
15. 440.46 pounds
16. 4,487.08 pounds
17. 1,561.13 pounds
18. 690.1 pounds

19. 19,890.4 pounds
20. 453.43 pounds
21. 400 pounds
22. 150 pounds
23. 133 pounds
24. 400 pounds
25. 200 pounds
26. 240 pounds

Chapter 3:
Mechanical Advantage

Calculating Mechanical Advantage and Mechanical Disadvantage

To calculate the overall mechanical advantage of a system, we often trace the forces on the line (or lines) and the compare the weight being supported to the force needed to support it.

Example:

Answers

1. 66.67 pounds   4. 33.33 pounds   7. 16.67 pounds

2. 33.33 pounds   5. 33.33 pounds   8. 16.67 pounds

3. 33.33 pounds   6. 16.67 pounds   9. 6:1

Problems

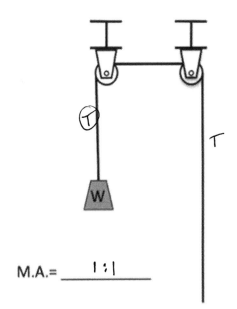

M.A.= ___1 : 1___

System 1

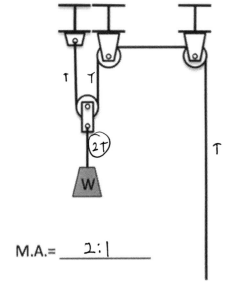

M.A.= ___2 : 1___

System 2

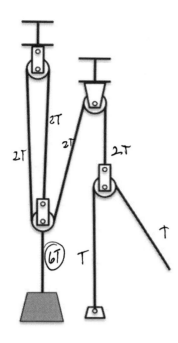

M.A.= __6:1__

System 3

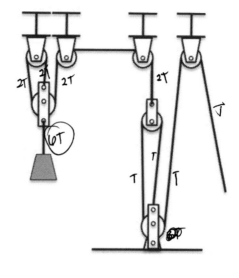

M.A.= __6:1__

System 4

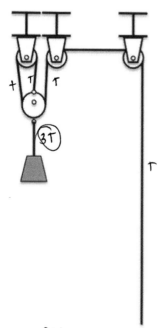

M.A.= __3:1__

System 5

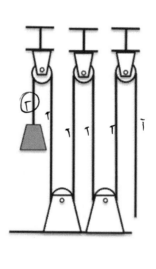

M.A.= __1:1__

System 6

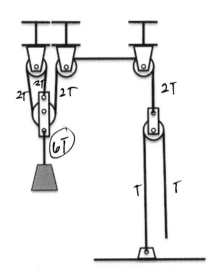

M.A.= _____4:1_____

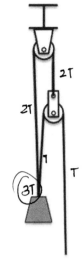

M.A.= _____3:1_____

System 7

System 8

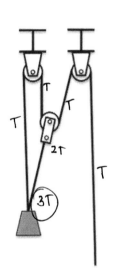

M.A.= _____3:1_____

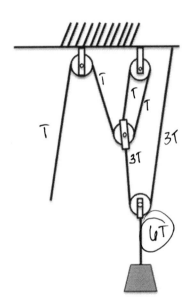

M.A.= _____6:1_____

System 9

System 10

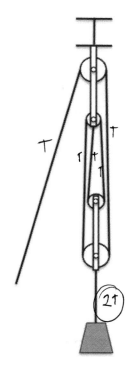

M.A.= __2:1__

System 11

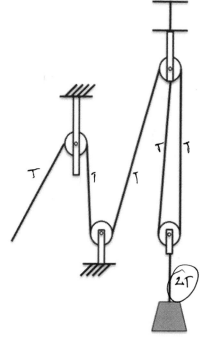

M.A.= __2:1__

System 12

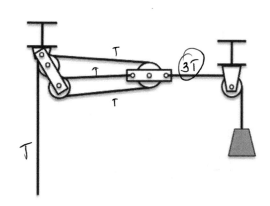

M.A.= __3:1__

System 13

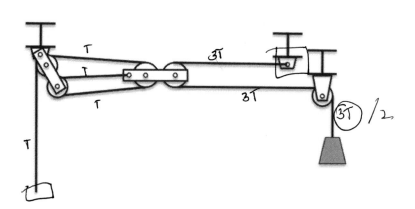

M.A.= __3:2__

System 14

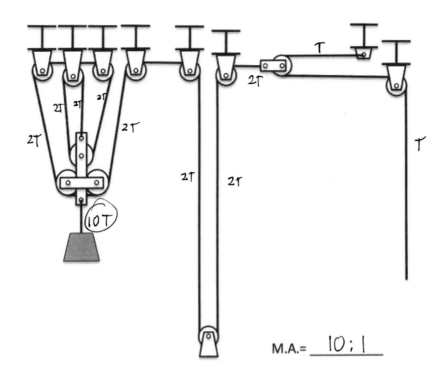

M.A.= __10:1__

System 15

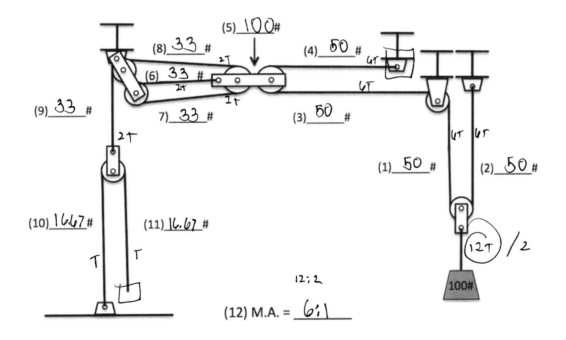

(5) __100__ #

(8) __33__ #

(4) __50__ #

(6) __33__ #

(9) __33__ #

7) __33__ #

(3) __50__ #

(1) __50__ #

(2) __50__ #

(10) __16.67__ #

(11) __16.67__ #

12:2

(12) M.A. = __6:1__

System 16

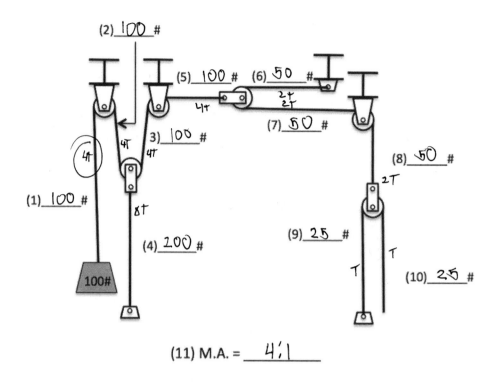

(2) __100__ #

(5) __100__ #   (6) __50__ #

2t
2t

4t

3) __100__ #   (7) __50__ #

(8) __50__ #

2T

(1) __100__ #

8t

(4) __200__ #

100#

(9) __25__ #

T

T

(10) __25__ #

(11) M.A. = __4:1__

System 17

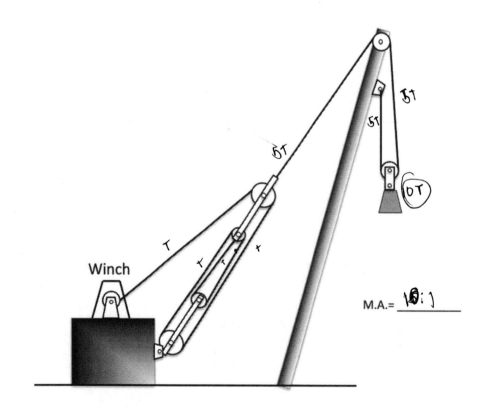

Winch

T

T   T   t

8t

5t

5t

0T

M.A.= __10:1__

System 18

Answers

1. 1:1	14. 3:2	16 (12). 6:1
2. 2:1	15. 10:1	17 (1). 100 pounds
3. 6:1	16 (1). 50 pounds	17 (2). 100 pounds
4. 6:1	16 (2). 50 pounds	17 (3). 100 pounds
5. 3:1	16 (3). 50 pounds	17 (4). 200 pounds
6. 1:1	16 (4). 50 pounds	17 (5). 100 pounds
7. 6:1	16 (5). 100 pounds	17 (6). 50 pounds
8. 3:1	16 (6). 33.33 pounds	17 (7). 50 pounds
9. 3:1	16 (7). 33.33 pounds	17 (8). 50 pounds
10. 6:1	16 (8). 33.33 pounds	17 (9). 25 pounds
11. 4:1	16 (9). 33.33 pounds	17 (10). 25 pounds
12. 2:1	16 (10). 16.67 pounds	17 (11). 4:1
13. 3:1	16 (11). 16.67 pounds	18. 10:1

Chapter 4:
Fleet Angles and D:d Ratios

This chapter covers:

Calculating the maximum offset distance for a 1.5 degree fleet angle

Calculating fleet angles (in degrees)

Calculating D:d ratios

Calculating the maximum offset distance

The formula for calculating the maximum allowable offset distance is:

Maximum Allowable Offset = Distance × .026

Example: What is the maximum allowable offset of a cable at 15 feet?

Maximum Allowable Offset = 15 × 0.026

Maximum Allowable Offset = 0.39 feet or 4.68 inches

Problems

1. What is the maximum allowable offset (in inches) for a cable at 39 feet?

2. What is the maximum allowable offset (in inches) for a cable at 12 feet?

3. What is the maximum allowable offset (in inches) of a cable at 20.5 feet?

4. What is the maximum allowable offset (in inches) of a cable at 87 feet?

5. What is the maximum allowable offset (in inches) of a cable at 102 feet?

6. What is the maximum allowable offset (in inches) of a cable at 76 feet?

7. What is the maximum allowable offset (in inches) of a cable at 83 feet?

8. What is the maximum allowable offset (in inches) of a cable at 56.7 feet?

9. What is the maximum allowable offset (in inches) of a cable at 38 feet?

10. What is the maximum allowable offset (in inches) of a cable at 22.3 feet?

11. What is the maximum allowable offset (in inches) of a cable at 12.4 feet?

12. What is the maximum allowable offset (in inches) of a cable at 24 feet?

13. What is the maximum allowable offset (in inches) of a cable at 10.3 feet?

14. What is the maximum allowable offset (in inches) of a cable at 30.6 feet?

15. What is the maximum allowable offset (in inches) of a cable at 132 feet?

16. What is the maximum allowable offset (in inches) of a cable at 85.4 feet?

17. What is the maximum allowable offset (in inches) of a cable at 41 feet?

18. What is the maximum allowable offset (in inches) of a cable at 18 feet?

19. What is the maximum allowable offset (in inches) of a cable at 0.45 feet?

20. What is the maximum allowable offset (in inches) of a cable at 48.9 feet?

Answers

Calculating the maximum offset distance

1. 12.168 inches
2. 3.7439 inches
3. 6.3960 inches
4. 27.144 inches
5. 31.823 inches
6. 23.712 inches
7. 25.896 inches
8. 17.690 inches

9. 11.856 inches
10. 6.9575 inches
11. 3.8688 inches
12. 7.4879 inches
13. 32.135 inches
14. 9.5472 inches
15. 41.184 inches
16. 26.644 inches

17. 12.792 inches
18. 5.616 inches
19. 0.1404 inches
20. 15.256 inches

Calculating a fleet angle

The formula for calculating a fleet angle is:

$$Angle = Arctangent \; of \; \left(\frac{Offset \; Distance}{Measurement \; Distance} \right)$$

Example: What is the fleet angel of a cable whose offset distance is 8" (0.666667 feet) at a distance of 35 feet?

$$Fleet \; Angle = Arctangent \; of \; \left(\frac{0.666667}{35} \right)$$

Fleet Angle = Arctangent of 0.019047619

Fleet Angle = 1.09 degrees

Problems

1. What is the fleet angle of a cable whose offset is 10" at 38 feet?

2. What is the fleet angle of a cable whose offset is 2" at 12.5 feet?

3. What is the fleet angle of a cable whose offset is 14.5" at 70 feet?

4. What is the fleet angle of a cable whose offset is 8" at 18 feet?

5. What is the fleet angle of a cable whose offset is 14" at 56 feet?

6. What is the fleet angle of a cable whose offset is 19" at 26 feet?

7. What is the fleet angle of a cable whose offset is 11" at 47 feet?

8. What is the fleet angle of a cable whose offset is 9" at 32 feet?

9. What is the fleet angle of a cable whose offset is 6" at 13 feet?

10. What is the fleet angle of a cable whose offset is 15" at 22 feet?

11. What is the fleet angle of a cable whose offset is 2" at 33 feet?

12. What is the fleet angle of a cable whose offset is 12" at 18 feet?

13. What is the fleet angle of a cable whose offset is 1.4" at 6 feet?

14.   What is the fleet angle of a cable whose offset is 3.2" at 19.5 feet?

15.   What is the fleet angle of a cable whose offset is 8.5" at 14.3 feet?

16.   What is the fleet angle of a cable whose offset is 5" at 26 feet?

17.   What is the fleet angle of a cable whose offset is 7" at 10 feet?

18.   What is the fleet angle of a cable whose offset is 3.3" at 19 feet?

19.   What is the fleet angle of a cable whose offset is 6.5" at 22 feet?

20.   What is the fleet angle of a cable whose offset is 1.1" at 8.2 feet?

Answers

Calculating a fleet angle

1. 1.2562 degrees

2. 0.7638 degrees

3. 0.9889 degrees

4. 2.1210 degrees

5. 1.1934 degrees

6. 3.4848 degrees

7. 1.1173 degrees

8. 1.3426 degrees

9. 2.2025 degrees

10. 3.2519 degrees

11. 0.2893 degrees

12. 3.1798 degrees

13. 1.1139 degrees

14. 0.7834 degrees

15. 2.8357 degrees

16. 0.9181 degrees

17. 3.3384 degrees

18. 0.8292 degrees

19. 1.4104 degrees

20. 0.640 degrees

Calculating D:d Ratios

Example 1: What is the minimum recommended sheave diameter that should be used with a ¼"
diameter 7x19 GAC, assuming a minimum D:d ratio of 30:1?

Sheave diameter = $30 \times 1/4$"

Sheave diameter = 30/4

Sheave diameter = 7.5 inches

Example 2: If the sheave has a 3" diameter and the wire rope in it is 1/8" what is the D:d ratio?

D:d ratio = $3 / 0.125 : 1$

D:d ratio = 24 : 1

Problems

1. What is the minimum recommended sheave diameter that should be used with a 3/32" diameter 7x19 GAC, assuming a minimum D:d ratio of 30:1?

2. What is the minimum recommended sheave diameter that should be used with a 1/8" diameter 7x19 GAC, assuming a minimum D:d ratio of 30:1?

3. What is the minimum recommended sheave diameter that should be used with a 1/2" diameter 7x19 GAC, assuming a minimum D:d ratio of 30:1?

4. What is the minimum recommended sheave diameter that should be used with a 3/8" diameter 7x19 GAC, assuming a minimum D:d ratio of 30:1?

5. What is the minimum recommended sheave diameter that should be used with a 3/4" diameter 7x19 GAC, assuming a minimum D:d ratio of 30:1?

6. What is the minimum recommended sheave diameter that should be used with a 7/8" diameter 7x19 GAC, assuming a minimum D:d ratio of 30:1?

7. What is the minimum recommended sheave diameter that should be used with a 5/32" diameter 7x19 GAC, assuming a minimum D:d ratio of 30:1?

8. What is the minimum recommended sheave diameter that should be used with a 1/16" diameter 7x19 GAC, assuming a minimum D:d ratio of 30:1?

9. What is the minimum recommended sheave diameter that should be used with a 1/2" diameter fiber rope, assuming a minimum D:d ratio of 8:1?

10. What is the minimum recommended sheave diameter that should be used with a 1/4" diameter fiber rope, assuming a minimum D:d ratio of 8:1?

11. What is the minimum recommended sheave diameter that should be used with a 3/4" diameter fiber rope, assuming a minimum D:d ratio of 8:1?

12. What is the minimum recommended sheave diameter that should be used with a 3/32" diameter fiber rope, assuming a minimum D:d ratio of 8:1?

13. What is the minimum recommended sheave diameter that should be used with a 1/4" diameter 7x7 GAC wire rope, assuming a minimum D:d ratio of 40:1?

14. What is the minimum recommended sheave diameter that should be used with a 7/8" diameter 7x7 GAC wire rope, assuming a minimum D:d ratio of 40:1?

15. What is the minimum recommended sheave diameter that should be used with a 1/8" diameter7x7 GAC wire rope, assuming a minimum D:d ratio of 40:1?

16. What is the minimum recommended sheave diameter that should be used with a 7/16" diameter 7x7 GAC wire rope, assuming a minimum D:d ratio of 40:1?

17. What is the minimum recommended sheave diameter that should be used with a 1/2" diameter 7x7 GAC wire rope, assuming a minimum D:d ratio of 40:1?

18. What is the minimum recommended sheave diameter that should be used with a 5/32" diameter 7x7 GAC wire rope, assuming a minimum D:d ratio of 40:1?

19. What is the minimum recommended sheave diameter that should be used with a 3/4" diameter 6x41 Warrington Seale wire rope, assuming a suggested D:d ratio of 32:1?

20. What is the minimum recommended sheave diameter that should be used with a 3/4" diameter 8x25 tiller wire rope, assuming a minimum D:d ratio of 21:1?

Answers

Calculating a D:d ratio

1. 2.8125 inches
2. 3.75 inches
3. 15 inches
4. 11.25 inches
5. 22.5 inches
6. 26.25 inches
7. 4.6875 inches

8. 1.875 inches
9. 4 inches
10. 2 inches
11. 6 inches
12. 0.75 inches
13. 10 inches
14. 35 inches

15. 5 inches
16. 17.5 inches
17. 20 inches
18. 6.25 inches
19. 24 inches
20. 16 inches

Unit III:
Bridles

Chapter 5:
Two-Point Bridles

This chapter focus on calculating bridle lengths and angles.

<u>Calculating Bridle Lengths</u>

The formula for calculating length of each leg of the bridle is:

$$Bridle\ Length\ of\ Leg\ =\ \sqrt{Horizontal\ Distance^2\ +\ Vertical\ Distance^2}\ \ or$$

$$L1 = \sqrt{H1^2 + V1^2}\ \ and\ \ L2 = \sqrt{H2^2 + V2^2}$$

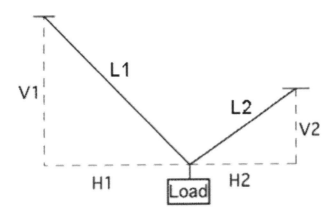

Example: Calculate the lengths of L1 and L2 where, V1 = 10', H1 = 4', V2 = 6, and H2 = 3'.

$$L1 = \sqrt{10^2 + 4^2}$$

$$L1 = \sqrt{100 + 16}$$

$$L1 = \sqrt{116}$$

$$L1 = 10.77\ feet$$

and

$$L1 = \sqrt{6^2 + 3^2}$$

$$L1 = \sqrt{36 + 9}$$

$$L1 = \sqrt{45}$$

$$L1 = 6.7 \text{ feet}$$

Problems

1. Calculate the lengths of both legs of a bridle (L1 and L2) where V1 is 22', H1 is 20', V2 is 18' and H2 is 14'.

2. Calculate the lengths of both legs of a bridle (L1 and L2) where V1 is 8', H1 is 6', V2 is 12' and H2 is 6'.

3. Calculate the lengths of both legs of a bridle (L1 and L2) where V1 is 13', H1 is 10', V2 is 13' and H2 is 10'.

4. Calculate the lengths of both legs of a bridle (L1 and L2) where V1 is 26', H1 is 12', V2 is 18' and H2 is 20'.

5. Calculate the lengths of both legs of a bridle (L1 and L2) where V1 is 24.4', H1 is 11', V2 is 18.9' and H2 is 8'.

6. Calculate the lengths of both legs of a bridle (L1 and L2) where V1 is 102', H1 is 46.3', V2 is 93.5' and H2 is 32.5'.

7. Calculate the lengths of both legs of a bridle (L1 and L2) where V1 is 89.4', H1 is 44', V2 is 89.4' and H2 is 32.5'.

8. Calculate the lengths of both legs of a bridle (L1 and L2) where V1 is 33.6', H1 is 28.6', V2 is 30.4' and H2 is 12.8'.

9. Calculate the lengths of both legs of a bridle (L1 and L2) where V1 is 20.9', H1 is 9.2', V2 is 33.6' and H2 is 10.7'.

10. Calculate the lengths of both legs of a bridle (L1 and L2) where V1 is 55.4', H1 is 20.6', V2 is 87.3' and H2 is 25.3'.

11. Calculate the lengths of both legs of a bridle (L1 and L2) where V1 is 9.4', H1 is 4', V2 is 10' and H2 is 4'.

12. Calculate the lengths of both legs of a bridle (L1 and L2) where V1 is 66', H1 is 10.5', V2 is 66' and H2 is 11.7'.

13. Calculate the lengths of both legs of a bridle (L1 and L2) where V1 is 26.3', H1 is 11', V2 is 36.1' and H2 is 9'.

14. Calculate the lengths of both legs of a bridle (L1 and L2) where V1 is 55', H1 is 30', V2 is 49' and H2 is 23.3'.

15. Calculate the lengths of both legs of a bridle (L1 and L2) where V1 is 205', H1 is 56.5', V2 is 196' and H2 is 49.2'.

16. Calculate the lengths of both legs of a bridle (L1 and L2) where V1 is 23', H1 is 10.4', V2 is 23' and H2 is 12.6'.

17. Calculate the lengths of both legs of a bridle (L1 and L2) where V1 is 44.9', H1 is 26.5', V2 is 37' and H2 is 26.5'.

18. Calculate the lengths of both legs of a bridle (L1 and L2) where V1 is 50', H1 is 24', V2 is 46' and H2 is 18'.

19. Calculate the lengths of both legs of a bridle (L1 and L2) where V1 is 44', H1 is 18.4', V2 is 44' and H2 is 12.8'.

20. Calculate the lengths of both legs of a bridle (L1 and L2) where V1 is 76', H1 is 22.4', V2 is 78' and H2 is 20.01'.

Answers

1. L1=29.732 and L2=22.803

2. L1=10 and L2=13.416

3. L1=16.401 and L2=16.401

4. L1=28.635 and L2=26.907

5. L1=26.764 and L2=20.523

6. L1=112.01 and L2= 98.987

7. L1=99.641 and L2=95.124

8. L1=44.123 and L2=32.984

9. L1=2.835 and L2=35.262

10. L1=59.106 and L2=90.892

11. L1=10.215 and L2=10.770

12. L1=66.830 and L2=67.029

13. L1=28.507 and L2=37.204

14. L1=62.649 and L2=54.257

15. L1=212.64 and L2=202.08

16. L1=25.242 and L2=26.225

17. L1=52.136 and L2=45.510

18. L1=55.461 and L2=49.396

19. L1=47.692 and L2=45.824

20. L1=79.232 and L2=80.54

Calculating the Bridle Angle

The equation for calculating the angle between the two bridle legs is:

$$Angle = \left(Arctangent\left(\frac{H1}{V1}\right)\right) + \left(Arctangent\left(\frac{H2}{V2}\right)\right)$$

Example: What is the bridle angle, where V1 = 10', H1 = 4', V2 = 6, and H2 = 3'?

$$Angle = \left(Arctangent\left(\frac{4}{10}\right)\right) + \left(Arctangent\left(\frac{3}{6}\right)\right)$$

$$Angle = \left(Arctangent\left(0.4\right)\right) + \left(Arctangent\left(0.5\right)\right)$$

Angle = 21.8 + 26.56

Angle = 48.36 degrees

Problems

1. Calculate the angle between bridles L1 and L2 if V1 is 22', H1 is 20', V2 is 18' and H2 is 14'.

2. Calculate the angle between bridles L1 and L2 if V1 is 8', H1 is 6', V2 is 12' and H2 is 6'.

3. Calculate the angle between bridles L1 and L2 if V1 is 13', H1 is 10', V2 is 13' and H2 is 10'.

4. Calculate the angle between bridles L1 and L2 if V1 is 26', H1 is 12', V2 is 18' and H2 is 20'.

5. Calculate the angle between bridles L1 and L2 if where V1 is 24.4', H1 is 11', V2 is 18.9' and H2 is 8'.

6. Calculate the angle between bridles L1 and L2 if where V1 is 102', H1 is 46.3', V2 is 93.5' and H2 is 32.5'.

7. Calculate the angle between bridles L1 and L2 if V1 is 89.4', H1 is 44', V2 is 89.4' and H2 is 32.5'.

8. Calculate the angle between bridles L1 and L2 if V1 is 33.6', H1 is 28.6', V2 is 30.4' and H2 is 12.8'.

9. Calculate the angle between bridles L1 and L2 if V1 is 20.9', H1 is 9.2', V2 is 33.6' and H2 is 10.7'.

10. Calculate the angle between bridles L1 and L2 if V1 is 55.4', H1 is 20.6', V2 is 87.3' and H2 is 25.3'.

11. Calculate the angle between bridles L1 and L2 if V1 is 9.4', H1 is 4', V2 is 10' and H2 is 4'.

12. Calculate the angle between bridles L1 and L2 if V1 is 66', H1 is 10.5', V2 is 66' and H2 is 11.7'.

13. Calculate the angle between bridles L1 and L2 if V1 is 26.3', H1 is 11', V2 is 36.1' and H2 is 9'.

14. Calculate the angle between bridles L1 and L2 if V1 is 55', H1 is 30', V2 is 49' and H2 is 23.3'.

15. Calculate the angle between bridles L1 and L2 if V1 is 205', H1 is 56.5', V2 is 196' and H2 is 49.2'.

16. Calculate the angle between bridles L1 and L2 if V1 is 23', H1 is 10.4', V2 is 23' and H2 is 12.6'.

17. Calculate the angle between bridles L1 and L2 if V1 is 44.9', H1 is 26.5', V2 is 37' and H2 is 26.5'.

18. Calculate the angle between bridles L1 and L2 if V1 is 50', H1 is 24', V2 is 46' and H2 is 18'.

19. Calculate the angle between bridles L1 and L2 if V1 is 44', H1 is 18.4', V2 is 44' and H2 is 12.8'.

20. Calculate the angle between bridles L1 and L2 if V1 is 76', H1 is 22.4', V2 is 78' and H2 is 20.01'.

Answers

1. 80.1 degrees

2. 63.4 degrees

3. 75.1 degrees

4. 72.8 degrees

5. 47.2 degrees

6. 43.6 degrees

7. 46.2 degrees

8. 63.2 degrees

9. 41.4 degrees

10. 36.6 degrees

11. 44.8 degrees

12. 19.1 degrees

13. 36.7 degrees

14. 54 degrees

15. 29.5 degrees

16. 53 degrees

17. 66.2 degrees

18. 47degrees

19. 38.9 degrees

20. 30.8 degrees

Chapter 6:

Tension on Bridle Legs

To compute the tension on the two bridles, we use the equations

$$Tension\ on\ L1 = Load\ \times\ \frac{L1 \times H2}{(V1 \times H2) + (V2 \times H1)}$$

$$Tension\ on\ L2 = Load\ \times\ \frac{L2 \times H1}{(V1 \times H2) + (V2 \times H1)}$$

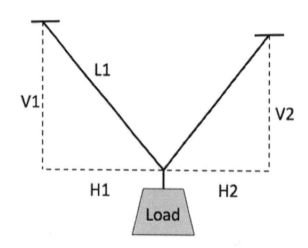

Example: Calculate the tension on L1 and L2 based on the following information:

L1 = 5'   L2 = 6.7'
V1 = 4'   V2 = 3'
H1 = 3'   H2 = 6'
Load = 500 lb

Note: in the problems at the end of this chapter, you will not given the lengths of L1 or L2. You must calculate these using H1 and V1, and H2 and V2, just as you did in Chapter 5.

$$Tension\ on\ L1 = 500 \times \frac{5 \times 6}{(4 \times 6) + (3 \times 3)}$$

$$Tension\ on\ L1 = 500 \times \frac{30}{24 + 9}$$

$$Tension\ on\ L1 = 500 \times \frac{30}{33}$$

$$Tension\ on\ L1 = 500 \times 0.9090909$$

$$Tension\ on\ L1 = 454.545\ pounds$$

$$Tension\ on\ L2 = 500 \times \frac{6.7 \times 3}{(4 \times 6) + (3 \times 3)}$$

$$Tension\ on\ L2 = 500 \times \frac{20.1}{24 + 9}$$

$$Tension\ on\ L2 = 500 \times \frac{20.1}{33}$$

$$Tension\ on\ L2 = 500 \times 0.6090909$$

$$Tension\ on\ L2 = 304.545\ pounds$$

Problems

1. Calculate the tension on the bridles L1 and L2 where V1 is 22', H1 is 20', V2 is 18' and H2 is 14'. The load is 300 lb.

2. Calculate the tension on the bridles L1 and L2 where V1 is 8', H1 is 6', V2 is 12' and H2 is 6'. The load is 850 lb.

3. Calculate the tension on the bridles L1 and L2 where V1 is 13', H1 is 10', V2 is 13' and H2 is 10'. The load is 475 lb.

4. Calculate the tension on the bridles L1 and L2 where V1 is 26', H1 is 12', V2 is 18' and H2 is 20'. Load is 1079 lb.

5. Calculate the tension on the bridles L1 and L2 where V1 is 24.4', H1 is 11', V2 is 18.9' and H2 is 8'. Load is 734.5 lb

6. Calculate the tension on the bridles L1 and L2 where V1 is 102', H1 is 46.3', V2 is 93.5' and H2 is 32.5'. Load is 1000 lb.

7. Calculate the tension on the bridles L1 and L2 where V1 is 89.4', H1 is 44', V2 is 89.4' and H2 is 32.5'. Load is 888 lb.

8. Calculate the tension on the bridles L1 and L2 where V1 is 33.6', H1 is 28.6', V2 is 30.4' and H2 is 12.8'. Load is 394.3 lb.

9. Calculate the tension on the bridles L1 and L2 where V1 is 20.9', H1 is 9.2', V2 is 33.6' and H2 is 10.7'. Load is 729.3 lb.

10. Calculate the tension on the bridles L1 and L2 where V1 is 55.4', H1 is 20.6', V2 is 87.3' and H2 is 25.3'. Load is 560 lb.

11. Calculate the tension on the bridles L1 and L2 where V1 is 9.4', H1 is 4', V2 is 10' and H2 is 4'. Load is 2050 lb

12. Calculate the tension on the bridles L1 and L2 where V1 is 66', H1 is 10.5', V2 is 66' and H2 is 11.7'. Load is 5000 lb.

13. Calculate the tension on the bridles L1 and L2 where V1 is 26.3', H1 is 11', V2 is 36.1' and H2 is 9'. Load is 5699 lb.

14. Calculate the tension on the bridles L1 and L2 where V1 is 55', H1 is 30', V2 is 49' and H2 is 23.3'. Load is 1100 lb.

15. Calculate the tension on the bridles L1 and L2 where V1 is 205', H1 is 56.5', V2 is 205' and H2 is 49.2'. Load is 7500 lb.

16. Calculate the tension on the bridles L1 and L2 where V1 is 23', H1 is 10.4', V2 is 23' and H2 is 12.6'. Load is 3400 lb.

17. Calculate the tension on the bridles L1 and L2 where V1 is 44.9', H1 is 26.5', V2 is 37' and H2 is 26.5'. Load is 468 lb.

18. Calculate the tension on the bridles L1 and L2 where V1 is 50', H1 is 24', V2 is 46' and H2 is 18'. Load is 988.5 lb.

19. Calculate the tension on the bridles L1 and L2 where V1 is 44', H1 is 18.4', V2 is 44' and H2 is 12.8'. Load is 555 lb.

20 Calculate the tension on the bridles L1 and L2 where V1 is 76', H1 is 22.4', V2 is 78' and H2 is 20'. Load is 4099 lb.

Answers

1. L1 = 186.928 lb, L2 = 204.821 lb
2. L1 = 425.000 lb, L2 = 570.197 lb
3. L1 = 299.637 lb, L2 = 299.637 lb
4. L1 = 839.615 lb, L2 = 473.362 lb
5. L1 = 390.152 lb, L2 = 411.359 lb
6. L1 = 476.257 lb, L2 = 599.566 lb
7. L1 = 420.471 lb, L2 = 543.447 lb
8. L1 = 171.367 lb, L2 = 286.236 lb
9. L1 = 334.482 lb, L2 = 444.104 lb
10. L 1= 261.691 lb, L2 = 327.666 lb
11. L1 = 1,079.49 lb, L2 = 1,138.10 lb
12. L1 = 2,668.27 lb, L2 = 2401.73 lb
13. L1 = 2,307.02 lb, L2 = 3,679.93 lb
14. L1 = 583.578 lb, L2 = 650.736 lb
15. L1 = 3,621.17 lb, L2 = 4,122.83 lb
16. L1 = 2,044.17 lb, L2 = 1,752.97 lb
17. L1 = 297.952 lb, L2 = 260.062 lb
18. L1 = 492.430 lb, L2 = 584.770 lb
19. L1 = 246.799 lb, L2 = 340.876 lb
20. L1 = 1,988.08 lb, L2 = 2,262.93 lb

Chapter 7:

Tension on a Horizontal Breastline

Calculating the tension on a horizontal breastline

The equation for calculating horizontal force on a breastline is:

$$Horizontal\ Force = Load \times \frac{H1}{V1}$$

Below is a diagram of this configuration.

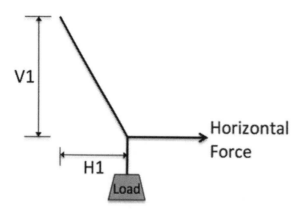

Example: Calculate the horizontal force on a breastline where V1 is 30', H1 is 2', and the Load = 700 pounds.

$$\text{Horizontal Force} = \text{Load} \times \frac{2}{30}$$

$$\text{Horizontal Force} = \text{Load} \times 0.0666$$

$$\text{Horizontal Force} = 700 \times 0.0666$$

$$\text{Horizontal Force} = 46.62 \text{ lb}$$

Problems

1. Calculate the horizontal force on a breastline where V1 is 30', H1 is 8', and the Load = 800 lb.

2. Calculate the horizontal force on a breastline where V1 is 25', H1 is 12', and the Load = 350 lb.

3. Calculate the horizontal force on a breastline where V1 is 18', H1 is 14', and the Load = 400 lb.

4. Calculate the horizontal force on a breastline where V1 is 45', H1 is 23', and the Load = 1,000 lb.

5. Calculate the horizontal force on a breastline where V1 is 23.5', H1 is 8.9', and the Load = 1,500 lb.

6. Calculate the horizontal force on a breastline where V1 is 35', H1 is 7', and the Load = 700 lb.

7. Calculate the horizontal force on a breastline where V1 is 100', H1 is 40', and the Load = 550 lb.

8. Calculate the horizontal force on a breastline where V1 is 48', H1 is 15', and the Load = 560 lb.

9. Calculate the horizontal force on a breastline where V1 is 34', H1 is 16', and the Load = 1,200lb.

10. Calculate the horizontal force on a breastline where V1 is 45', H1 is 45', and the Load = 1,200 lb.

11. Calculate the horizontal force on a breastline where V1 is 76', H1 is 34.4', and the Load = 570 lb.

12. Calculate the horizontal force on a breastline where V1 is 98.4', H1 is 22.6', and the Load = 350 lb.

13. Calculate the horizontal force on a breastline where V1 is 376, H1 is 201', and the Load =780 lb.

14. Calculate the horizontal force on a breastline where V1 is 99', H1 is 56.3', and the Load = 376 lb.

15. Calculate the horizontal force on a breastline where V1 is 423', H1 is 164', and the Load = 567 lb.

16. Calculate the horizontal force on a breastline where V1 is 33.5', H1 is 7', and the Load = 125.5 lb.

17. Calculate the horizontal force on a breastline where V1 is 65.3', H1 is 44', and the Load = 434 lb.

18. Calculate the horizontal force on a breastline where V1 is 69', H1 is 54.3', and the Load = 1,543 lb.

19. Calculate the horizontal force on a breastline where V1 is 54', H1 is 50', and the Load = 6,707 lb.

20. Calculate the horizontal force on a breastline where V1 is 77', H1 is 44.7', and the Load = 5,100 lb.

Answers

1. 213.333 lb	8. 175.00 lb	15. 219.829 lb
2. 168.00 lb	9. 564.705 lb	16. 26.2238 lb
3. 311.111 lb	10. 1200.0 lb	17. 292.434 lb
4. 511.111 lb	11. 258.00 lb	18. 1214.27 lb
5. 568.085 lb	12. 122.357 lb	19. 6210.18 lb
6. 140.00 lb	13. 416.968 lb	20. 2960.64 lb
7. 220.00 lb	14. 213.826 lb	

Chapter 8:

Three-Point Bridle Lengths

Calculating Three-point Bridle Lengths

Always begin by collecting and organizing the data below.

P1   X: _____   Y: _____   Z: _____

P2   X: _____   Y: _____   Z: _____

P3   X: _____   Y: _____   Z: _____

P4   X: _____   Y: _____   Z: _____

Note: P1, P2, and P3 will be the hanging points for our three bridle legs (L1, L2 and L3) and P4 will be the bridle point (where the three legs meet). Z is the height of the point.

When you have this data, use the equations below for calculating the lengths of the three bridle legs (L1, L2 and L3) are:

$$L1 = \sqrt{(X1 - X4)^2 + (Y1 - Y4)^2 + (Z1 - XZ4)^2}$$

$$L2 = \sqrt{(X2 - X4)^2 + (Y2 - Y4)^2 + (Z2 - XZ4)^2}$$

$$L3 = \sqrt{(X3 - X4)^2 + (Y3 - Y4)^2 + (Z3 - XZ4)^2}$$

Example: Using the data below, calculate the lengths of L1, L2 and L3.

P1   X1: __0__   Y1: __0__   Z1: __50__

P2   X2: __0__   Y2: __12__   Z2: __50__

P3   X3: __16__   Y3: __6__   Z3: __50__

P4   X4: __8__   Y4: __7__   Z4: __35__

$$L1 = \sqrt{(X1 - X4)^2 + (Y1 - Y4)^2 + (Z1 - XZ4)^2}$$

$$L1 = \sqrt{(0 - 8)^2 + (0 - 7)^2 + (50 - 35)^2}$$

$$L1 = \sqrt{(-8)^2 + (-7)^2 + (15)^2}$$

$$L1 = \sqrt{64 + 49 + 225}$$

$$L1 = \sqrt{338}$$

$$L1 = 18.38 \text{ feet}$$

$$L2 = \sqrt{(X2 - X4)^2 + (Y2 - Y4)^2 + (Z2 - XZ4)^2}$$

$$L1 = \sqrt{(0 - 8)^2 + (12 - 7)^2 + (50 - 35)^2}$$

$$L2 = \sqrt{(-8)^2 + (5)^2 + (15)^2}$$

$$L2 = \sqrt{64 + 25 + 225}$$

$$L2 = \sqrt{314}$$

$$L2 = 17.72 \text{ feet}$$

$$L3 = \sqrt{(X3 - X4)^2 + (Y3 - Y4)^2 + (Z3 - XZ4)^2}$$

$$L3 = \sqrt{(16 - 8)^2 + (6 - 7)^2 + (50 - 35)^2}$$

$$L3 = \sqrt{(-8)^2 + (-1)^2 + (15)^2}$$

$$L3 = \sqrt{64 + 1 + 225}$$

$$L3 = \sqrt{290}$$

$$L3 = 17.03 \text{ feet}$$

Another Method for Calculating Three-point Bridle Lengths

Rigging Math Made Simple, Second Edition explains a second method of calculating the lengths of three-point bridles. This method involves first calculating the horizontal distances from the the hanging points (P1, P2 and P3) to the bridle point (P4) using the Pythagorean theorem. Then using each of these distances, along with the other two, to calculate the length of each bridle leg (again, using the Pythagorean theorem.

Example: Using the data from the drawing below, calculate the length of L1.

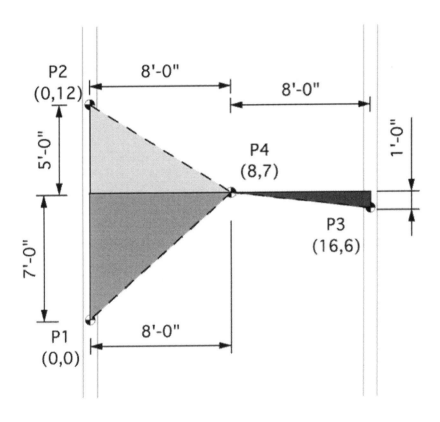

$$H1 = \sqrt{8^2 + 7^2}$$

$$H1 = \sqrt{64 + 49}$$

$$H1 = \sqrt{113}$$

$$H1 = 10.63 \text{ feet}$$

$$L1 = \sqrt{10.63^2 + 15^2}$$

$$L1 = \sqrt{113 + 225}$$

$$L1 = \sqrt{338}$$

$$L1 = 18.38 \text{ feet}$$

The lengths of L2 and L3 would be calculated in a similar fashion.

Problems

1. Using the data below, calculate the lengths of L1, L2 and L3.

P1   X1: ___0___   Y1: ___3___   Z1: ___60___

P2   X2: ___22___   Y2: ___0___   Z2: ___60___

P3   X3: ___12___   Y3: ___24___   Z3: ___60___

P4   X4: ___12___   Y4: ___12___   Z4: ___35___

2. Using the data below, calculate the lengths of L1, L2 and L3.

P1   X1: ___10.5___   Y1: ___1___   Z1: ___70___

P2   X2: ___22___   Y2: ___14___   Z2: ___70___

P3   X3: ___5___   Y3: ___19___   Z3: ___70___

P4   X4: ___9.5___   Y4: ___13___   Z4: ___36___

3. Using the data below, calculate the lengths of L1, L2 and L3.

P1   X1: __4____   Y1: __4____   Z1: ____50____

P2   X2: __20___   Y2: __2____   Z2: ____50____

P3   X3: __14___   Y3: __18___   Z3: ____50____

P4   X4: __14___   Y4: __13___   Z4: ____23____

4. Using the data below, calculate the lengths of L1, L2 and L3.

P1   X1: __2___   Y1: ___8____   Z1: ___23___

P2   X2: __18.5_   Y2: ___1____   Z2: ___23___

P3   X3: __14___   Y3: ___20____   Z3: ___23___

P4   X4: __13___   Y4: ___12____   Z4: ___8____

5. Using the data below, calculate the lengths of L1, L2 and L3.

P1   X1: __2___   Y1: ___4___   Z1: __35___

P2   X2: __12__   Y2: ___0___   Z2: __35___

P3   X3: __19___   Y3: __22____   Z3: __35____

P4   X4: __5___   Y4: __11___   Z4: __20____

6. Using the data below, calculate the lengths of L1, L2 and L3.

P1   X1: __8___   Y1: __10__   Z1: __63___

P2   X2: __36___   Y2: __0___   Z2: __55___

P3   X3: __29___   Y3: __42___   Z3: __79___

P4   X4: __15___   Y4: __15___   Z4: __35___

7. Using the data below, calculate the lengths of L1, L2 and L3.

P1   X1: __2____   Y1: __33___   Z1: __78___

P2   X2: __10___   Y2: __4___   Z2: __72___

P3   X3: __40___   Y3: __21___   Z3: __79___

P4   X4: __14.5__   Y4: __11___   Z4: __42___

8. Using the data below, calculate the lengths of L1, L2 and L3.

P1   X1: __0____   Y1: __0___   Z1: __80___

P2   X2: __20___   Y2: __0___   Z2: __80___

P3   X3: __0____   Y3: __9____   Z3: __80___

P4   X4: __6____   Y4: __5____   Z4: __32___

9. Using the data below, calculate the lengths of L1, L2 and L3.

P1   X1: __3____   Y1: __17.5___ Z1: __67___

P2   X2: __38____   Y2: __3_____   Z2: __67___

P3   X3: __29____   Y3: __24_____ Z3: __63___

P4   X4: __17____   Y4: __15_____ Z4: __30___

10. Using the data below, calculate the lengths of L1, L2 and L3.

P1   X1: __10____   Y1: __4_____ Z1: __56___

P2   X2: __11___   Y2: __25_____ Z2: __56___

P3   X3: __31___   Y3: __20_____ Z3: __56___

P4   X4: __23____   Y4: __20_____ Z4: __33___

11. Using the data below, calculate the lengths of L1, L2 and L3.

P1   X1: __2__   Y1: __0__   Z1: __47__

P2   X2: __0__   Y2: __18__   Z2: __54__

P3   X3: __15__   Y3: __5__   Z3: __51__

P4   X4: __8__   Y4: __7__   Z4: __22__

12. Using the data below, calculate the lengths of L1, L2 and L3.

P1   X1: __4__   Y1: __29__   Z1: __55__

P2   X2: __11__   Y2: __8.4__   Z2: __55__

P3   X3: __43.2__   Y3: __22__   Z3: __55__

P4   X4: __14__   Y4: __10__   Z4: __39__

13. Using the data below, calculate the lengths of L1, L2 and L3.

P1   X1: __12__   Y1: __3.6__   Z1: __60__

P2   X2: __10.2__   Y2: __25.7__   Z2: __58__

P3   X3: __29__   Y3: __22.6__   Z3: __61__

P4   X4: __24.3__   Y4: __20__   Z4: __40__

14. Using the data below, calculate the lengths of L1, L2 and L3.

P1   X1: __4__   Y1: __0__   Z1: __82__

P2   X2: __25__   Y2: __21__   Z2: __82__

P3   X3: __0__   Y3: __20__   Z3: __82__

P4   X4: __5__   Y4: __12.5__   Z4: __52__

15. Using the data below, calculate the lengths of L1, L2 and L3.

P1   X1: __12__   Y1: __2__   Z1: __60__

P2   X2: __30__   Y2: __21__   Z2: __60__

P3   X3: __6.2__   Y3: __25__   Z3: __60__

P4   X4: __16__   Y4: __14__   Z4: __48__

16. Using the data below, calculate the lengths of L1, L2 and L3.

P1   X1: __16.5__   Y1: __3__   Z1: __25__

P2   X2: __25__   Y2: __23__   Z2: __25__

P3   X3: __2__   Y3: __19__   Z3: __25__

P4   X4: __15__   Y4: __12__   Z4: __18__

17. Using the data below, calculate the lengths of L1, L2 and L3.

P1   X1: __0__   Y1: __0__   Z1: __49__

P2   X2: __10__   Y2: __10__   Z2: __49__

P3   X3: __20__   Y3: __0__   Z3: __49__

P4   X4: __10__   Y4: __4__   Z4: __30__

18. Using the data below, calculate the lengths of L1, L2 and L3.

P1   X1: __5__   Y1: __0__   Z1: __90__

P2   X2: __40__   Y2: __4__   Z2: __90__

P3   X3: __16__   Y3: __37__   Z3: __90__

P4   X4: __12__   Y4: __15__   Z4: __75__

19. Using the data below, calculate the lengths of L1, L2 and L3.

P1   X1: __0___   Y1: __0___   Z1: __75___

P2   X2: __37___   Y2: __14___   Z2: __75___

P3   X3: __0___   Y3: __35___   Z3: __75___

P4   X4: __15___   Y4: __13___   Z4: __48___

20. Using the data below, calculate the lengths of L1, L2 and L3.

P1   X1: __-9__   Y1: __-6__   Z1: __50___

P2   X2: __8__   Y2: __-5___   Z2: __50___

P3   X3: __-4___   Y3: __9__   Z3: __50___

P4   X4: __0__   Y4: __0___   Z4: __40___

Answers

1. L1= 29.154 ft, L2= 29.478 ft, L3= 27.730 ft

2. L1= 36.224 ft, L2= 34.942 ft, L3= 35.679 ft

3. L1= 30.166 ft, L2= 29.765 ft, L3= 27.459 ft

4 L1= 19.026 ft, L2= 19.397 ft, L3= 17.029 ft

5. L1= 16.822 ft, L2= 19.874 ft, L3= 23.280 ft

6. L1= 29.291 ft. L2= 32.649 ft. L3= 53.488 ft

7. L1= 44.002 ft, L2= 31.132 ft, L3= 46.035 ft

8. L1= 48.631 ft, L2= 50.249 ft, L3= 48.538 ft

9. L1= 39.638 ft, L2= 44.204 ft, L3= 36.249 ft

10. L1= 30.886 ft, L2= 26.419 ft, L3= 24.351 ft

11. L1= 26.645 ft, L2= 34.770 ft, L3= 29.899 ft

12. L1= 26.776 ft, L2= 16.357 ft, L3= 35.392 ft

13. L1= 28.640 ft, L2= 23.564 ft, L3= 21.676 ft

14. L1= 32.515 ft, L2= 37.043 ft, L3= 31.324 ft

15. L1= 17.435 ft, L2= 19.723 ft, L3= 19.001 ft

16. L1= 11.50 ft. L2= 16.431 ft, L3= 16.340 ft

17. L1= 21.840 ft, L2= 19.924 ft, L3= 21.840 ft

18. L1=22.338 ft, L2= 33.615 ft, L3= 26.925 ft

19. L1= 33.511 ft, L2= 34.842 ft, L3= 37.920 ft

20. L1= 14.730 ft, L2=13.747 ft, L3= 14.035 ft

Chapter 9:

Tension on Three-Point Bridles

Calculating the tension on three-point bridle, by hand, is an extremely complex and tedious task. While one method of doing this type of calculation is demonstrated in Rigging Math Made Simple, Second Edition, it is not something that we actually recommend riggers attempt. We strongly recommend that riggers use an app like *RigCalc* or a computer application for making these types of calculation.

Problems

Calculate the tensions on the bridle legs using *RigCalc*.

1. Using the data below, calculate the bridle tension on L1, L2 and L3. Load is 1,000 lb.

P1   X1: ___0___   Y1: ___3___   Z1: ___60___

P2   X2: __22___   Y2: ___0___   Z2: ___60___

P3   X3: __12___   Y3: __24___   Z3: ___60___

P4   X4: __12___   Y4: __12___   Z4: ___35___

2. Using the data below, calculate the bridle tension on L1, L2 and L3. Load is 800 lb.

P1   X1: __10.5___   Y1: ___1___   Z1: ___70___

P2   X2: __22___   Y2: __14___   Z2: ___70___

P3   X3: ___5___   Y3: __19___   Z3: ___70___

P4   X4: __9.5___   Y4: __13___   Z4: ___36___

3. Using the data below, calculate the bridle tension on L1, L2 and L3. Load is 1,500 lb.

P1   X1: __4____   Y1: __4____   Z1: ____50____

P2   X2: __20___   Y2: __2____   Z2: ____50____

P3   X3: __14___   Y3: __18___   Z3: ____50____

P4   X4: __14___   Y4: __13___   Z4: ____23____

4. Using the data below, calculate the bridle tension on L1, L2 and L3. Load is 500 lb.

P1   X1: __2___   Y1: ___8____   Z1: ____23____

P2   X2: __18.5_   Y2: ___1____   Z2: ____23____

P3   X3: __14___   Y3: ___20____   Z3: ____23____

P4   X4: __13___   Y4: ___12____   Z4: ___8____

5. Using the data below, calculate the bridle tension on L1, L2 and L3. Load is 395 lb.

P1   X1: __12____   Y1: __3.6____   Z1: __60___

P2   X2: __10.2___   Y2: __25.7___   Z2: __58___

P3   X3: __29_____   Y3: __22.6___   Z3: __61___

P4   X4: __24.3____   Y4: __20____   Z4: __40___

6. Using the data below, calculate the bridle tension on L1, L2 and L3. Load is 1,205 lb.

P1   X1: __8____   Y1: __10__   Z1: __63___

P2   X2: __36___   Y2: __0___   Z2: __55___

P3   X3: __29___   Y3: __42___   Z3: __79___

P4   X4: __15___   Y4: __15___   Z4: __35___

7. Using the data below, calculate the bridle tension on L1, L2 and L3. Load is 2,045 lb.

P1   X1: __2__   Y1: __33__   Z1: __78__

P2   X2: __10__   Y2: __4__   Z2: __72__

P3   X3: __40__   Y3: __21__   Z3: __79__

P4   X4: __14.5__   Y4: __11__   Z4: __42__

8. Using the data below, calculate the bridle tension on L1, L2 and L3. Load is 902 lb.

P1   X1: __0__   Y1: __0__   Z1: __80__

P2   X2: __20__   Y2: __0__   Z2: __80__

P3   X3: __0__   Y3: __9__   Z3: __80__

P4   X4: __6__   Y4: __5__   Z4: __32__

9. Using the data below, calculate the bridle tension on L1, L2 and L3. Load is 422 lb.

P1   X1: __3__   Y1: __17.5__   Z1: __67__

P2   X2: __38__   Y2: __3__   Z2: __67__

P3   X3: __29__   Y3: __24__   Z3: __63__

P4   X4: __17__   Y4: __15__   Z4: __30__

10. Using the data below, calculate the bridle tension on L1, L2 and L3. Load is 1,222 lb.

P1   X1: __10__   Y1: __4__   Z1: __56__

P2   X2: __11__   Y2: __25__   Z2: __56__

P3   X3: __31__   Y3: __20__   Z3: __56__

P4   X4: __23__   Y4: __20__   Z4: __33__

Answers

1. Tension L1 = 281.009 lb, Tension L2 = 340.959 lb, Tension L3 = 521.206 lb

2. Tension L1 = 242.265 lb, Tension L2 = 146.960 lb, Tension L3 = 444.179 lb

3. Tension L1 = 206.053 lb, Tension L2 = 338.863 lb, Tension L3 = 1,025.33 lb

4. Tension L1 = 123.693 lb, Tension L2 = 192.595 lb, Tension L3 = 287.848 lb

5. Tension L1 = 85.3590 lb, Tension L2 = 49.9212 lb, Tension L3 = 306.828 lb

6. Tension L1 = 821.707 lb, Tension L2= 140.274 lb, Tension L3 = 405.537 lb

7. Tension L1 = 372.078 lb, Tension L2 = 1,352.74 lb, Tension L3 = 543.803 lb

8. Tension L1 = 132.002 lb, Tension L2 = 283.280 lb, Tension L3 = 506.734 lb

9. Tension L1 = 254.299 lb, Tension L2 = 132.851 lb, Tension L3 = 80.6601 lb

10. Tension L1 = 154.450 lb, Tension L2 = 422.758 lb, Tension L3 = 782.374 lb

Unit IV:
Truss

Chapter 10:

Center of Gravity for Two Loads on a Beam

The diagram below shows this type of problem.

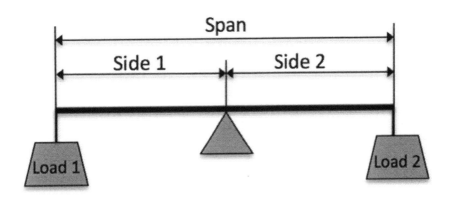

The equations to solve this problem are:

$$Length\ of\ Side\ 1 = \frac{Load\ 2 \times Span}{Load\ 1 + Load\ 2}$$

$$Length\ of\ Side\ 2 = \frac{Load\ 1 \times Span}{Load\ 1 + Load\ 2}$$

or

$Length\ of\ Side\ 2 = Span - Length\ of\ Side\ 1$

Example: If the total span is 10 feet, and Load 1 is 150 lb and Load 2 is 100 lb, where is the center of gravity (what are the lengths of Side 1 and Side 2)?

$$\text{Length of Side 1} = \frac{\text{Load 2} \times \text{Span}}{\text{Load 1} + \text{Load 2}}$$

$$\text{Length of Side 1} = \frac{100 \times 10}{150 + 100}$$

$$\text{Length of Side 1} = \frac{1000}{250}$$

Length of Side 1 = 4 feet

$$\text{Length of Side 2} = \frac{\text{Load 1} \times \text{Span}}{\text{Load 1} + \text{Load 2}}$$

$$\text{Length of Side 2} = \frac{150 \times 10}{150 + 100}$$

$$\text{Length of Side 2} = \frac{1500}{250}$$

Length of Side 2 = 6 feet

or

Length of Side 2 = Span – Length of Side 1

Length of Side 2 = 10 – 4

Length of Side 2 = 6 feet

Problems

1. If the Span is 30', and Load 1= 300 lb and Load 2= 200 lb, what are the lengths of Side 1 and Side 2?

2. If the Span is 40', and Load 1= 600 lb and Load 2= 250 lb, what are the lengths of Side 1 and Side 2?

3. If the Span is 35', and Load 1= 342 lb and Load 2= 832 lb, what are the lengths of Side 1 and Side 2?

4. If the Span is 105', and Load 1= 892 lb and Load 2= 524 lb, what are the lengths of Side 1 and Side 2?

5. If the Span is 80', and Load 1= 492 lb and Load 2= 1,034 lb, what are the lengths of Side 1 and Side 2?

6. If the Span is 8.2', and Load 1= 254.3 lb and Load 2= 851.6 lb, what are the lengths of Side 1 and Side 2?

7. If the Span is 43', and Load 1= 673.45 lb and Load 2= 23.55 lb, what are the lengths of Side 1 and Side 2?

8. If the Span is 100', and Load 1= 75.65 lb and Load 2= 44.87 lb, what are the lengths of Side 1 and Side 2?

9. If the Span is 177.33', and Load 1= 5,455 lb and Load 2= 4,378 lb, what are the lengths of Side 1 and Side 2?

10. If the Span is 20', and Load 1= 300.59 lb and Load 2= 342.56 lb, what are the lengths of Side 1 and Side 2?

11. If the Span is 45', and Load 1= 654 lb and Load 2= 443.5 lb, what are the lengths of Side 1 and Side 2?

12. If the Span is 50.5', and Load 1= 639 lb and Load 2= 237 lb, what are the lengths of Side 1 and Side 2?

13. If the Span is 300', and Load 1= 5,033 lb and Load 2= 2,443 lb, what are the lengths of Side 1 and Side 2?

14. If the Span is 75', and Load 1= 2,452.5 lb and Load 2= 2,387.4 lb, what are the lengths of Side 1 and Side 2?

15. If the Span is 177', and Load 1= 765.66 lb and Load 2= 734.88 lb, what are the lengths of Side 1 and Side 2?

16. If the Span is 13.7', and Load 1= 406.55 lb and Load 2= 2,009 lb, what are the lengths of Side 1 and Side 2?

17. If the Span is 65', and Load 1= 310.56 lb and Load 2= 237.83 lb, what are the lengths of Side 1 and Side 2?

18. If the Span is 90', and Load 1= 762.5 lb and Load 2= 2,567.5 lb, what are the lengths of Side 1 and Side 2?

19. If the Span is 125', and Load 1= 2,300.44 lb and Load 2= 3,422.98 lb, what are the lengths of Side 1 and Side 2?

20. If the Span is 255', and Load 1= 338.73 lb and Load 2= 4,034.55 lb, what are the lengths of Side 1 and Side 2?

Answers

1. Side 1= 12 ft, Side 2= 18 ft
2. Side 1= 11.76 ft, Side 2= 28.23 ft
3. Side 1= 24.80 ft, Side 2= 10.20 ft
4. Side 1= 38.86 ft, Side 2= 66.14 ft
5. Side 1= 54.20 ft, Side 2= 25.79 ft
6. Side 1= 6.31 ft, Side 2= 1.89 ft
7. Side 1= 1.45ft, Side 2= 41.55 ft
8. Side 1= 37.23 ft, Side 2= 62.77 ft
9. Side 1= 78.95 ft, Side 2= 98.38 ft
10. Side 1= 10.65 ft, Side 2= 9.35 ft

11. Side 1= 18.18 ft, Side 2= 26.82 ft
12. Side 1= 13.66 ft, Side 2= 36.84 ft
13. Side 1= 98.03 ft, Side 2= 201.97 ft
14. Side 1= 37.00 ft, Side 2= 38.00 ft
15. Side 1= 86.68 ft, Side 2= 90.32 ft
16. Side 1= 11.39 ft, Side 2= 2.31 ft
17. Side 1= 28.19 ft, Side 2= 36.81 ft
18. Side 1= 69.39 ft, Side 2= 20.61 ft
19. Side 1= 74.76 ft, Side 2= 50.24 ft
20. Side 1= 235.25 ft, Side 2= 19.75 ft

Chapter 11:

Uniformly Distributed Loads on a Beam

When a load is evenly distributed across the entire length of a truss or batten the percentage of the load on the points can vary greatly. The diagram below provides a simplified method for determining the load on each point.

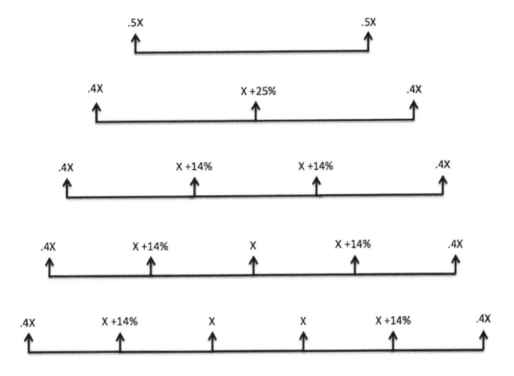

Reprinted with permission from Harry Donovan's, *Entertainment Rigging: A Practical Guide, Chapter 16, Page 14.*

"X" is the total weight of the load, divided by the number of segments of beam. The number of segments is the number of supporting lines minus one. So, for a beam supported by three lines, there are two segments; for a beam supported by four lines, there are three segments; for a beam supported by five lines, there are four segments; etc.

Example: If a UDL of 1,500 pounds is dead hung from a batten that is supported by three equally spaced lift lines, calculate the load on each line.

$X = 1,500 / 2$ (three minus one)

$X = 750$ lb

So,

$L1 = 750 \times 0.4 = 300$ lb

$L2 = 750 + 25\%$ of 750 (187.5) $= 937.5$ lb

$L3 = 750 \times 0.4 = 300$ lb

Problems

1. If a UDL of 1,800 lb is dead hung from a batten that is supported by four equally spaced lift lines, what is the load on each line?

2. If a UDL of 2,200 lb is dead hung from a batten that is supported by two equally spaced lift lines, what is the load on each line?

3. If a UDL of 3,400 lb is dead hung from a batten that is supported by five equally spaced lift lines, what is the load on each line?

4. If a UDL of 10,000 lb is dead hung from a batten that is supported by eight equally spaced lift lines, what is the load on each line?

5. If a UDL of 5,500 lb is dead hung from a batten that is supported by six equally spaced lift lines, what is the load on each line?

6. If a UDL of 2,600 lb is dead hung from a batten that is supported by four equally spaced lift lines, what is the load on each line?

7. If a UDL of 3,800 lb is dead hung from a batten that is supported by seven equally spaced lift lines, what is the load on each line?

8. If a UDL of 1,598 lb is dead hung from a batten that is supported by three equally spaced lift lines, what is the load on each line?

9. If a UDL of 800 lb is dead hung from a batten that is supported by five equally spaced lift lines, what is the load on each line?

10. If a UDL of 1,864.5 lb is dead hung from a batten that is supported by four equally spaced lift lines, what is the load on each line?

11. If a UDL of 3,055.6 lb is dead hung from a batten that is supported by seven equally spaced lift lines, what is the load on each line?

12. If a UDL of 8,450 lb is dead hung from a batten that is supported by eight equally spaced lift lines, what is the load on each line?

13. If a UDL of 534.3 lb is dead hung from a batten that is supported by two equally spaced lift lines, what is the load on each line?

14. If a UDL of 1,690 lb is dead hung from a batten that is supported by three equally spaced lift lines, what is the load on each line?

15. If a UDL of 7,632 lb is dead hung from a batten that is supported by five equally spaced lift lines, what is the load on each line?

16. If a UDL of 9,304 lb is dead hung from a batten that is supported by six equally spaced lift lines, what is the load on each line?

17. If a UDL of 468.36 lb is dead hung from a batten that is supported by four equally spaced lift lines, what is the load on each line?

18. If a UDL of 6,500.5 lb is dead hung from a batten that is supported by seven equally spaced lift lines, what is the load on each line?

19. If a UDL of 2,305 lb is dead hung from a batten that is supported by five equally spaced lift lines, what is the load on each line?

20. If a UDL of 7,770 lb is dead hung from a batten that is supported by six equally spaced lift lines, what is the load on each line?

Answers

1. Points 1 & 4 = 240 lb each, Points 2 & 3 = 684 lb each

2. Points 1 & 2 = 1,100 lb each

3. Points 1 & 5 = 340 lb each, Points 2 & 4 = 969 lb each, Point 3 = 850 lb

4. Points 1 & 8 = 571 lb each, Points 2 &7 = 1,629 lb each, and Points 3, 4, 5, 6 = 1,429 lb each

5. Points 1 & 6 = 440 lb each, Points 2 &5 = 1,254 lb each, and Points 3 & 4 = 1,100 lb each

6. Points 1 & 4 = 346.7 lb each, Points 2 & 3 = 988 lb each

7. Points 1 & 7 = 253.3 lb each, Points 2 &6 = 722 lb each, and Points 3, 4, 5 = 633.3 lb each

8. Points 1 & 3 = 319.6 lb each, Point 2 = 998.8 lb

9. Points 1 & 5 = 80 lb each, Points 2 & 4= 228 lb each, and Point 3 = 200 lb each

10. Points 1 & 4 = 248.6 lb each, Points 2 & 3 = 708.51 lb each

11. Points 1 & 7 = 203.7 lb each, Points 2 & 6 = 580.6 lb each, and Points 3, 4, 5 = 509.3 lb each

12. Points 1 & 8 = 483 lb each, Points 2 & 7 = 1376 lb each, and Points 3, 4, 5, 6 = 1,207 lb each

13. Points 1 & 2 = 267.15 lb each

14. Points 1 & 3 = 338 lb each, Point 2 = 1,056.25 lb

15. Points 1 & 5 = 763.2 lb each, Points 2 & 4= 2,175.12 lb each, and Point 3 = 1,908 lb each

16. Points 1 & 6 = 744.32 lb each, Points 2 & 5 = 2,121.31 lb each, and Points 3 & 4 = 1,860.8 lb each

17. Points 1 & 4 = 62.448 lb each, Points 2 & 3 = 177.97 lb each

18. Points 1 & 7 = 433.36 lb each, Points 2 & 6 = 1,235.0 lb each, and Points 3, 4, 5 = 1,083.4 lb each

19. Points 1 & 5 = 230.5 lb each, Points 2 & 4 = 656.92 lb each, and Point 3 = 576.25 lb each

20. Points 1 & 6 = 621.6 lb each, Points 2 & 5 = 1,771.56 lb each, and Points 3 & 4 = 1,554 lb each

Chapter 12:

Dead-hang Tension on One End of a Truss

When the hanging point is not directly over the end of the truss, the tension on the leg is not the same as the (vertical) downward force at the end of the truss.

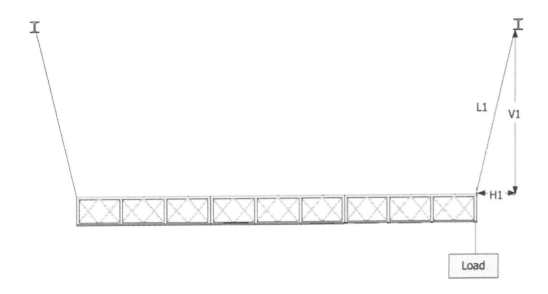

The equation to solve this problem type of problem is:

$$Tension\ on\ L1 = Load \times \frac{L1}{V1}$$

Note: In this problem we are ignoring the weight of the truss. The weight of the truss will be addressed in Lesson 16.

Example: If H1 = 4', V1 =10', and the Load = 400 lb, what is the tension on L1?

The first thing to do is to calculate the length of L1.

$$L1 = \sqrt{10^2 + 4^2}$$

$$L1 = \sqrt{100 + 16}$$

$$L1 = \sqrt{116}$$

$$L1 = 10.77 \text{ feet}$$

Now we put this length into the equation above and get:

$$\text{Tension on L1} = \text{Load} \times \frac{10.77}{10}$$

$$\text{Tension on L1} = 400 \times 1.077$$

$$\text{Tension on Leg L1} = 430.8 \text{ lb}$$

Problems

1. If H1 = 5', V1 =10', and the Load = 500 lb, what is the tension on L1?

2. If H1 = 6', V1 =18', and the Load = 700 lb, what is the tension on L1?

3. If H1 = 14', V1 =22', and the Load = 1,000 lb, what is the tension on L1?

4. If H1 = 22', V1 =22', and the Load = 1,800 lb, what is the tension on L1?

5. If H1 = 12.5', V1 =18.6', and the Load = 2,200 lb, what is the tension on L1?

6. If H1 = 17.3', V1 =36.4', and the Load = 3,400 lb, what is the tension on L1?

7. If H1 = 55', V1 =68.7', and the Load = 4,400 lb, what is the tension on L1?

8. If H1 = 28', V1 = 56', and the Load = 306.5 lb, what is the tension on L1?

9. If H1 = 8.8', V1 =10.2', and the Load = 5,42.5 lb, what is the tension on L1?

10. If H1 = 1.0', V1 =50', and the Load = 600 lb, what is the tension on L1?

11. If H1 = 0', V1 = 30', and the Load = 1,000 lb, what is the tension on L1?

12. If H1 = 5', V1 =1', and the Load = 1,000 lb, what is the tension on L1?

13. If H1 = 11.3', V1 =44.4', and the Load = 1800 lb, what is the tension on L1?

14. If H1 = 20', V1 =0', and the Load = 500 lb, what is the tension on L1?

15. If H1 = 46.2', V1 =100', and the Load = 2,312 lb, what is the tension on L1?

16. If H1 = 89', V1 = 208', and the Load = 2,500 lb, what is the tension on L1?

17. If H1 = 47.2', V1 = 42.3', and the Load = 480 lb, what is the tension on L1?

18. If H1 = 8.5', V1 = 39.4', and the Load = 843 lb, what is the tension on L1?

19. If H1 = 22.2', V1 = 49.3', and the Load = 453 lb, what is the tension on L1?

20. If H1 = 556', V1 =1032', and the Load = 498.5 lb, what is the tension on L1?

Answers

1. Tension on L1= 559.069 lb

2. Tension on L1= 737.868 lb

3. Tension on L1= 1,185.309 lb

4. Tension on L1= 2,545.584 lb

5. Tension on L1= 2,650.65 lb

6. Tension on L1= 3,764.471 lb

7. Tension on L1= 5,636.35 lb

8. Tension on L1= 342.6774 lb

9. Tension on L1= 716.4963 lb

10. Tension on L1= 600.1199 lb

11. Tension on L1= 1,000 lb

12. Tension on L1= 5,099.019 lb

13. Tension on L1= 1,857.38 lb

14. Tension on L1= "Infinity"

15. Tension on L1= 2,546.816 lb

16. Tension on L1= 2,719.243 lb

17. Tension on L1= 719.215 lb

18. Tension on L1= 862.3943 lb

19. Tension on L1= 496.8098 lb

20. Tension on L1= 566.2446 lb

Chapter 13:

Simple Load on a Beam

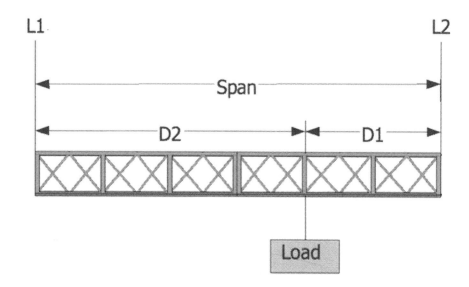

The formulas for solving this type are problem are.

$$Tension\ on\ L1 = \frac{Load \times D1}{Span}$$

Note: "You can also think of it as L1 = Load x (D1/Span) if that is easier for you to remember.

and

$$Tension\ on\ L2 = \frac{Load \times D2}{Span}$$

Note: You can also think of it as L2 = Load x (D2/Span) if that is easier for you to remember.

or

Tension on L2 = Load – L1

Example: If the Span is 20 feet, D1 is 5 feet and D2 is 15 feet (note: D1 + D2 must equal Span), and the Load 1 is 200 lb, what is the tension on L1 and L2?

$$\text{Tension on L1} = \frac{\text{Load} \times \text{D1}}{\text{Span}}$$

$$\text{Tension on L1} = \frac{200 \times 5}{20}$$

$$\text{Tension on L1} = \frac{1000}{20}$$

Tension on L1 = 50 lb

Reactions

$$0 = 20'(+L1) + \overset{5}{\cancel{6}}(-200)$$
$$0 = 20(L1) + {}^-1,000$$
$$\cancel{1},000 = 20(L1)$$
$$050\# = L1$$

and

$$\text{Tension on L2} = \frac{\text{Load} \times \text{D2}}{\text{Span}}$$

$$\text{Tension on L2} = \frac{200 \times 15}{20}$$

$$\text{Tension on L2} = \frac{3000}{20}$$

Tension on L2 = 150 lb

$$0 = 20'(-L2) + 15'(200)$$
$$0 = 20'(-L2) + 3,000$$
$$-3,000 = 20(-L2)$$
$$-150 = -L2$$
$$150\# = L2$$

Also, Tension on L1 + L2 must always equal the Load, which is one way to check your work. But, since that is true, once you find L1 you can compute the tension on L2 by using the simple equation Tension on L2 = Load – Tension on L1. Another easy check of your math is to make certain that the leg that is closest to the load has the most tension.

Problems

1. If the Span is 34', D1 is 5', D2 is 29' and the Load is 650 lb, what is the tension on L1 and L2?

2. If the Span is 20', D1 is 3', D2 is 17' and the Load is 400 lb, what is the tension on L1 and L2?

3. If the Span is 35', D1 is 8', D2 is 27' and the Load is 890 lb, what is the tension on L1 and L2?

4. If the Span is 80', D1 is 43', D2 is 37' and the Load is 570 lb, what is the tension on L1 and L2?

5. If the Span is 22', D1 is 6', D2 is 16' and the Load is 883 lb, what is the tension on L1 and L2?

6. If the Span is 16', D1 is 4', D2 is 12' and the Load is 388 lb, what is the tension on L1 and L2?

7. If the Span is 31', D1 is 8', D2 is 23' and the Load is 786 lb, what is the tension on L1 and L2?

8. If the Span is 24', D1 is 14', D2 is 10' and the Load is 580 lb, what is the tension on L1 and L2?

9. If the Span is 76', D1 is 34', D2 is 42' and the Load is 955 lb, what is the tension on L1 and L2?

10. If the Span is 44', D1 is 22', D2 is 22' and the Load is 733 lb, what is the tension on L1 and L2?

11. If the Span is 61', D1 is 42', D2 is 19' and the Load is 989 lb, what is the tension on L1 and L2?

12. If the Span is 88', D1 is 11', D2 is 77' and the Load is 4,700 lb, what is the tension on L1 and L2?

13. If the Span is 238', D1 is 54.6', D2 is 183.4' and the Load is 7,780 lb, what is the tension on L1 and L2?

14. If the Span is 500', D1 is 211', D2 is 289' and the Load is 520 lb, what is the tension on L1 and L2?

15. If the Span is 43.6', D1 is 22', D2 is 21.6' and the Load is 400 lb, what is the tension on L1 and L2?

16. If the Span is 71.9', D1 is 32.8', D2 is 39.1' and the Load is 3,289 lb, what is the tension on L1 and L2?

17. If the Span is 46', D1 is 18', D2 is 28' and the Load is 321.6 lb, what is the tension on L1 and L2?

18. If the Span is 15', D1 is 11', D2 is 4' and the Load is 4,055 lb, what is the tension on L1 and L2?

19. If the Span is 34', D1 is 13', D2 is 21' and the Load is 200.5 lb, what is the tension on L1 and L2?

20. If the Span is 45', D1 is 2', D2 is 43' and the Load is 2,465 lb, what is the tension on L1 and L2?

Answers

1. L1= 95.5882 lb, L2= 554.4117 lb

2. L1= 60 lb, L2= 340 lb

3. L1= 203.4285 lb, L2= 686.5714 lb

4. L1= 306.375 lb, L2= 263.625 lb

5. L1= 240.818 lb, L2= 642.181 lb

6. L1= 97 lb, L2=291 lb

7. L1= 202.838 lb, L2= 583.161 lb

8. L1= 338.333 lb, L2= 241.666 lb

9. L1= 427.236 lb, L2= 527.763 lb

10. L1= 366.5 lb, L2= 366.5 lb

11. L1= 680.950 lb, L2= 308.049 lb

12. L1= 587.5 lb, L2= 4,112.5 lb

13. L1= 1,784.82 lb, L2= 5,995.17 lb

14. L1= 219.44 lb, L2= 300.56 lb

15. L1= 201.834 lb, L2= 198.165 lb

16. L1= 1500.40 lb, L2= 1788.59 lb

17. L1= 125.843 lb, L2= 195.756 lb

18. L1= 2,973.66 lb, L2= 1,081.33 lb

19. L1= 76.6617 lb, L2= 123.838 lb

20. L1= 109.555 lb, L2= 2355.44 lb

Chapter 14:

Multiple Loads on a Beam

As in Chapter 13, our desire is to find the vertical force on the two supporting Legs (L1 and L2). The equations for solving this problem are:

$$Tension\ on\ L1 = \frac{(Load\ 1 \times D1) + (Load\ 2 \times D2)}{Span}$$

$$Tension\ on\ L2 = (Load\ 1 + Load\ 2) - Tension\ on\ L1$$

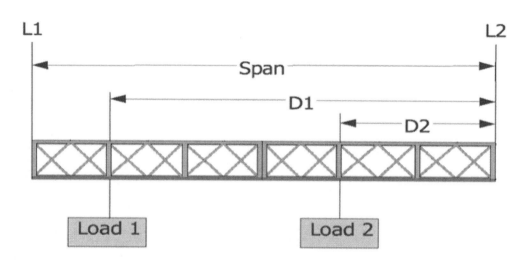

Example: If the Span is 20 feet, D1 is 17.5 feet, D2 is 5 feet, Load 1 is 100 lb and Load 2 is 200 lb, what is the tension on L1 and L2?

$$\text{Tension on L1} = \frac{(100 \times 17.5) + (200 \times 5)}{20}$$

$$\text{Tension on L1} = \frac{1750 + 1000}{20}$$

$$\text{Tension on L1} = \frac{2750}{20}$$

Tension on L1 = 137.5 pounds

and

Tension on L2= (100 + 200) - 137.5

Tension on L2= 300 - 137.5

Tension on L2 = 162.5 pounds

Problems

1. If the Span is 40', D1 is 20', D2 is 15, Load 1 is 300 lb and Load 2 is 900 lb, what is the tension on L1 and L2?

2. If the Span is 50', D1 is 18', D2 is 4', Load 1 is 500 lb and Load 2 is 1,000 lb, what is the tension on L1 and L2?

3. If the Span is 10', D1 is 8', D2 is 5', Load 1 is 650 lb and Load 2 is 322 lb, what is the tension on L1 and L2?

4. If the Span is 25', D1 is 10', D2 is 0', Load 1 is 321 lb and Load 2 is 845 lb, what is the tension on L1 and L2?

5. If the Span is 55', D1 is 10', D2 is 5', Load 1 is 310 lb and Load 2 is 430 lb, what is the tension on L1 and L2?

6. If the Span is 15', D1 is 14', D2 is 6', Load 1 is 555 lb and Load 2 is 298 lb, what is the tension on L1 and L2?

7. If the Span is 30', D1 is 24', D2 is 2.5', Load 1 is 845 lb and Load 2 is 823.5 lb, what is the tension on L1 and L2?

8. If the Span is 45', D1 is 38', D2 is 20', Load 1 is 493 lb and Load 2 is 1,348 lb, what is the tension on L1 and L2?

9. If the Span is 60', D1 is 43.8', D2 is 11.3', Load 1 is 1,928 lb and Load 2 is 2,098 lb, what is the tension on L1 and L2?

10. If the Span is 23.5', D1 is 19.2', D2 is 5.5', Load 1 is 609 lb and Load 2 is 194.8 lb, what is the tension on L1 and L2?

11. If the Span is 33.6', D1 is 29.7', D2 is 18.1', Load 1 is 2,845 lb and Load 2 is 1,930 lb, what is the tension on L1 and L2?

12. If the Span is 103', D1 is 98.4', D2 is 45', Load 1 is 1,376 lb and Load 2 is 3,423 lb, what is the tension on L1 and L2?

13. If the Span is 83.6', D1 is 48', D2 is 23.6, Load 1 is 1,543 lb and Load 2 is 1,005 lb, what is the tension on L1 and L2?

14. If the Span is 20', D1 is 20', D2 is 0', Load 1 is 300 lb and Load 2 is 600 lb, what is the tension on L1 and L2?

15. If the Span is 54.6', D1 is 22.4', D2 is 9.4', Load 1 is 432.6 lb and Load 2 is 546.7 lb, what is the tension on L1 and L2?

16. If the Span is 47.2', D1 is 40.2', D2 is 11.4', Load 1 is 985.4 lb and Load 2 is 445.4 lb, what is the tension on L1 and L2?

17. If the Span is 66.7', D1 is 66', D2 is 8', Load 1 is 598.8 lb and Load 2 is 342.4 lb, what is the tension on L1 and L2?

18. If the Span is 75', D1 is 67.6', D2 is 24.9', Load 1 is 884.9 lb and Load 2 is 443.2 lb, what is the tension on L1 and L2?

19. If the Span is 55', D1 is 49', D2 is 12', Load 1 is 335.8 lb and Load 2 is 493.9lb, what is the tension on L1 and L2?

20. If the Span is 110', D1 is 87.3', D2 is 36.3', Load 1 is 860 lb and Load 2 is 385.7 lb, what is the tension on L1 and L2?

Answers

1. L1 = 487.5 lb, L2 = 712.5 lb

2. L1 = 260 lb, L2 = 1240 lb

3. L1 = 681 lb, L2 = 291 lb

4. L1 = 128.4 lb, L2 = 1037.6 lb

5. L1 = 95.4545 lb, L2 = 644.545 lb

6. L1 = 637.2 lb, L2 = 215.8 lb

7. L1 = 744.625 lb, L2 = 923.875 lb

8. L1 = 1,015.42 lb, L2 = 825.577 lb

9. L1 = 1,802.56 lb, L2 = 2,223.43 lb

10. L1 = 543.157 lb, L2 = 260.642 lb

11. L1 = 3,554.44 lb, L2 = 1,220.55 lb

12. L1 = 2,810.03 lb, L2 = 1,988.96 lb

13. L1 = 1,169.64 lb, L2 = 1,378.35 lb

14. L1 = 300 lb, L2 = 600 lb

15. L1 = 271.597 lb, L2 = 707.702 lb

16. L1 = 946.835 lb, L2 = 483.964 lb

17. L1 = 633.583 lb, L2 = 307.616 lb

18. L1 = 944.732 lb, L2 = 383.367 lb

19. L1 = 406.927 lb, L2 = 422.772 lb

20. L1 = 809.808 lb, L2 = 435.891 lb

Chapter 15:
Cantilevered Load on a Beam

The equations for finding the tensions on L1 and L2 when you have a cantilevered load are:

$$Tension\ on\ L1 = \frac{(Load\ 1 \times D1) + (Load\ 2 \times D2) - (Load\ 3 \times D3)}{Span}$$

$$Tension\ on\ L2 = (Load1 + Load\ 2 + Load3) - L1$$

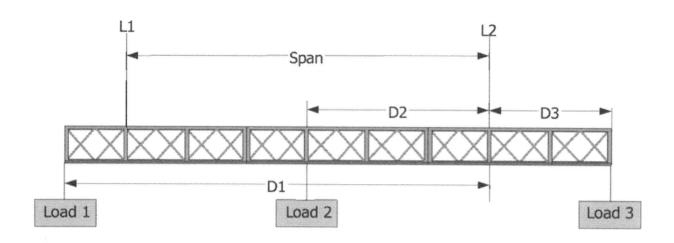

Example: If the Span is 40 feet, Load 1 is 200 lb, D1 is 30 feet, Load 2 is 150 lb, D2 is 10 feet, Load 3 is 100 lb, and D3 is 10 feet, what is the tension on L1 and L2?

$$Tension\ on\ L1 = \frac{(Load\ 1 \times D1) + (Load\ 2 \times D2) - (Load\ 3 \times D3)}{Span}$$

$$\text{Tension on L1} = \frac{(200 \times 30) + (150 \times \text{D2}) - (100 \times 10)}{40}$$

$$\text{Tension on L1} = \frac{(6000) + (1500) - 1000}{40}$$

$$\text{Tension on L1} = \frac{6500}{40}$$

Tension on L1 = 162.5 pounds

and

Tension on L2 = (200 + 150 + 100) - 162.5

Tension on L2 = 450 - 162.5

Tension on L2 = 287.5 pounds

Problems

1. If the Span is 30', D1 is 29', D2 is 9', D3 is 4', Load 1 is 400 lb, Load 2 is 300 lb and Load 3 is 500 lb, what is the tension on L1 and L2?

2. If the Span is 45', D1 is 35', D2 is 12', D3 is 5', Load 1 is 350 lb, Load 2 is 760 lb and Load 3 is 460 lb, what is the tension on L1 and L2?

3. If the Span is 25', D1 is 30', D2 is 5', D3 is 0', Load 1 is 600 lb, Load 2 is 800 lb and Load 3 is 500 lb, what is the tension on L1 and L2?

4. If the Span is 20', D1 is 28', D2 is 3', D3 is 2', Load 1 is 450 lb, Load 2 is 630 lb and Load 3 is 50 lb, what is the tension on L1 and L2?

5. If the Span is 40', D1 is 46', D2 is 11', D3 is 6', Load 1 is 435 lb, Load 2 is 784 lb and Load 3 is 338 lb, what is the tension on L1 and L2?

6. If the Span is 35', D1 is 35', D2 is 12', D3 is 5', Load 1 is 650 lb, Load 2 is 430 lb and Load 3 is 500 lb, what is the tension on L1 and L2?

7. If the Span is 40', D1 is 45', D2 is 16', D3 is 0', Load 1 is 698 lb, Load 2 is 443 lb and Load 3 is 983 lb, what is the tension on L1 and L2?

8. If the Span is 10', D1 is 15', D2 is 5', D3 is 5', Load 1 is 550 lb, Load 2 is 430 lb and Load 3 is 550 lb, what is the tension on L1 and L2?

9. If the Span is 25', D1 is 22', D2 is 8', D3 is 3', Load 1 is 800 lb, Load 2 is 500 lb and Load 3 is 300 lb, what is the tension on L1 and L2?

10. If the Span is 33', D1 is 35', D2 is 13', D3 is 8', Load 1 is 360 lb, Load 2 is 559 lb and Load 3 is 356 lb, what is the tension on L1 and L2?

11. If the Span is 55', D1 is 49', D2 is 44', D3 is 5', Load 1 is 600 lb, Load 2 is 700 lb and Load 3 is 344 lb, what is the tension on L1 and L2?

12. If the Span is 35', D1 is 33', D2 is 23', D3 is 8', Load 1 is 300 lb, Load 2 is 500 lb and Load 3 is 600 lb, what is the tension on L1 and L2?

13. If the Span is 24', D1 is 28', D2 is 15', D3 is 8', Load 1 is 105 lb, Load 2 is 659 lb and Load 3 is 100 lb, what is the tension on L1 and L2?

14. If the Span is 35', D1 is 41', D2 is 12', D3 is 8.5', Load 1 is 204 lb, Load 2 is 490 lb and Load 3 is 375 lb, what is the tension on L1 and L2?

15. If the Span is 22', D1 is 24.5', D2 is 20', D3 is 3.8', Load 1 is 904 lb, Load 2 is 328 lb and Load 3 is 590 lb, what is the tension on L1 and L2?

16. If the Span is 33.8', D1 is 44', D2 is 21', D3 is 4', Load 1 is 445 lb, Load 2 is 1923 lb and Load 3 is 459 lb, what is the tension on L1 and L2?

17. If the Span is 5', D1 is 8', D2 is 2.6', D3 is 4', Load 1 is 637 lb, Load 2 is 736 lb and Load 3 is 628 lb, what is the tension on L1 and L2?

18. If the Span is 60', D1 is 45', D2 is 10', D3 is 0', Load 1 is 847 lb, Load 2 is 309 lb and Load 3 is 930 lb, what is the tension on L1 and L2?

19. If the Span is 36.7', D1 is 43', D2 is 15', D3 is 6', Load 1 is 555 lb, Load 2 is 436 lb and Load 3 is 880 lb, what is the tension on L1 and L2?

20. If the Span is 58', D1 is 66', D2 is 23', D3 is 8', Load 1 is 814 lb, Load 2 is 543 lb and Load 3 is 112 lb, what is the tension on L1 and L2?

Answers

1. L1 = 410 lb, L2 = 790 lb

2. L1 = 423.777 lb, L2 = 1,146.22 lb

3. L1 = 880 lb, L2 = 1,020 lb

4. L1 = 719.5 lb, L2 = 410.5 lb.

5. L1 = 665.15 lb, L2 = 891.85 lb

6. L1 = 726 lb, L2 = 854 lb

7. L1 = 962.45 lb, L2 = 1,161.55 lb

8. L1 = 765 lb, L2 = 765 lb

9. L1 = 828 lb, L2 = 772 lb

10. L1 = 515.727 lb, L2 = 759.272 lb

11. L1 = 1,063.27 lb, L2 = 580.727 lb

12. L1 = 474.285 lb, L2 = 925.714 lb

13. L1 = 501.041 lb, L2 = 362.958 lb

14. L1 = 315.9 lb, L2 = 753.1 lb

15. L1 = 1,203 lb, L2 = 619 lb

16. L1 = 1,719.73 lb, L2 = 1,107.26 lb

17. L1 = 899.520 lb, L2 = 1,101.48 lb

18. L1 = 686.75 lb, L2 = 1,399.25 lb

19. L1 = 684.604 lb, L2 = 1,186.39 lb

20. L1 = 1,126.15 lb, L2 = 342.844 lb

Unit V:

Advanced Rigging

Chapter 16:

Chain Hoists and Truss and Lights. Oh my!

This chapter concentrates on calculating the load on the beams that support a truss and all of the things that technicians attach to a truss, as well as the chain hoist and chain that must be supported by the beams.   To solve the problems in this chapter, you will use some of the formulas covered in previous chapters.

Example 1: If the truss weight 10 pounds per foot, the curtain weights 300 pounds, the moving light weights 75 pounds, the chain hoist weights 120 pounds and the 50 feet of chain in each hoist weight 1 pound per foot, what is the load on points L1 and L2?

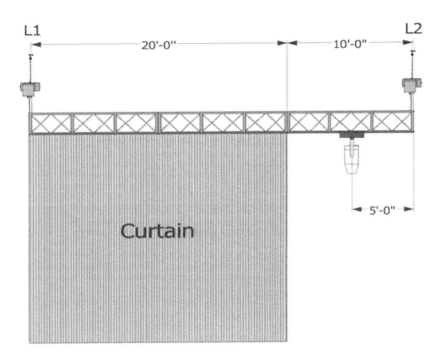

There are two Uniformly Distributed Loads on this rig: the truss itself and the curtain. The truss runs the entire span between the lift points, 30 feet, so half of the weight of the truss is on L1 and half on L2. If the truss weighs 10 pounds per linear foot, 300 pounds total, then both L1 and L2 have 150 pounds of tension on them so far.

The curtain is also a Uniformly Distributed Load, but only over 20 feet of the truss, starting with L1. A Uniformly Distributed Load can be converted into a single point load by finding its center of gravity. In this example, the center of gravity (or just the center of the curtain) is 10 feet from L1, or one-third of the span. If the curtain weighs 300 pounds, then 200 pounds of that load is on L1, and 100 pounds is on L2. So now: L1 = 150 + 200 = **350** pounds and L2 = 150 + 100 or **250** pounds.

Next, let's look at the Point Loads and calculate the distribution of the weight of one moving light hanging on the truss. This light, which weighs 75 pounds, is 5 feet from L2. We can use our basic point load equation to calculate the distribution of this load.

$$Tension\ on\ L1 = Load \times \frac{D1}{Span}$$

$$Tension\ on\ L1 = 75 \times \frac{5}{30}$$

$$Tension\ on\ L1 = 75 \times 0.1666$$

$$Tension\ on\ L1 = 12.5\ lb$$

$$Tension\ on\ L2 = Load - L1$$
$$Tension\ on\ L2 = 75 - 12.5$$
$$Tension\ on\ L2 = 62.5\ lb$$

Adding these numbers to our previous totals for L1 and L2, we get: L1 = 350 + 12.5 = 362.5 pounds and L2 = 250 + 62.5 = 312.5 pounds.

The last thing to add is the weight of the chain hoist and chain. These are also Point Loads, but since they are a part of the "leg" itself, their weight gets added directly to each leg. If a chain hoist weighs 120 pounds and there is 50 feet of chain, weighing one pound per foot, that form each "leg," then we add 170 pounds to both L1 and L2. So now, the tensions on the beams that support L1 and L2 are **532.5 pounds** and **482.5 pounds** respectively.

Example 2: If the truss weight 10 pounds per foot, the lights weights 15 pounds each, the three electrical cable weights 3 pounds per foot, the chain hoist weights 100 pounds and the 70 feet of chain in each hoist weight 1 pound per foot, what is the load on points L1, L2 and L3?

Note:
Electrical cable #1 runs from the center of the span between L1 and L2, to the SL end of the truss.
Electrical cable #2 runs from the center of the span between L2 and L3, to the SL end of the truss.
Electrical cable #3 runs from the center of the cantilevered truss section, to the SL end of the truss.
All three electrical cables then run from the SL end of the truss, to the floor.

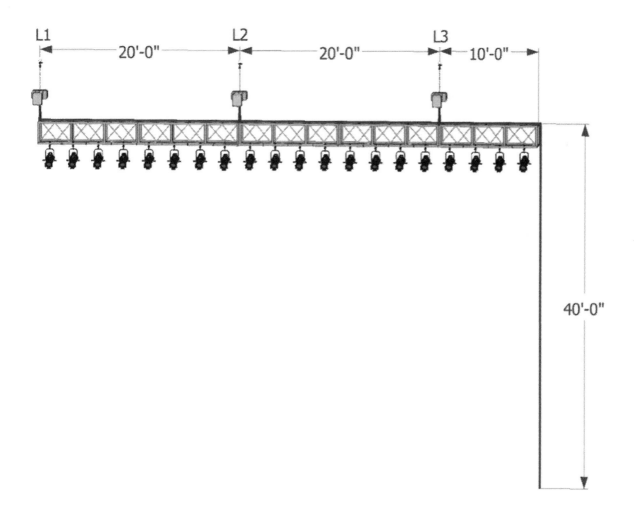

This rig has three uniformly distributed loads: the 50 feet of truss (10 pounds per foot), 20 Lekos (15 pounds each or 6 pounds per foot), and 50 feet of electrical cable (3 pounds per foot). There are also two point loads: each chain hoist and its 70 feet of chain (100 pounds per hoist and 1 pound per foot of chain), and the 40 feet of electrical cable that drops from the top of the truss to the floor (3 pounds per foot or 120 pounds of total weight). As before, we will keep a "running total" of the force on the three hanging points as we calculate them.

Both sections L1-L2 and L2-L3 have:

20 feet of truss at 10 pounds per foot	=	200 pounds
8 Lekos at 15 pounds each	=	120 pounds
	Total	320 pounds

Since we know that L1 and L3 are only supporting half of that load,

Tension on L1 = 160 lb
Tension on L2 = 320 lb
Tension on L3 = 160 lb

Now, let's deal with the weight that is cantilevered beyond H3. Since we know that this 10-foot of section of truss and the lights weigh half of our 20-foot long sections, it weighs 160 pounds. And because the load is uniformly distributed across those 10 feet, it is the same as 160 pounds being suspended at 5 feet from L3. So, doing the math, we get:

$$\text{Tension on L2} = -\text{Load} \times \frac{D1}{\text{Span}}$$

$$\text{Tension on L2} = -160 \times \frac{5}{20}$$

$$\text{Tension on L2} = -160 \times .25$$

$$\text{Tension on L2} = \text{-40 lb}$$

$$\text{Tension on L3} = \text{Load} - \text{L2}$$
$$\text{Tension on L3} = 160 - \text{-40}$$
$$\textbf{Tension on L3} = \textbf{200 lb}$$

So now,

Tension on L1 = 160 lb
Tension on L2 = 320 - 40 = 280 lb
Tension on L3 = 160 + 200 = 360 lb

Let's calculate the weight of the cables that are sitting on top of the truss, per section, next. Using the same formulas that we used above, we get:

	L1-L2	L2-L3	L3-SL end
EC#1	30 lb: L1= 7.5, L2=22.5	60 lb: L2=30, L3=30	30 lb: L2=-7.5, L3=37.5
EC#2	0	60 lb: L2=15, L3=45	30 lb: L2=-7.5, L3=37.5
EC#1	0	0	30 lb: L2=-5.625, L3=35.625

So,

Tension on L1 = 160 + 7.5 = 167.5 lb
Tension on L2 = 280 + 22.5 + 30 -7.5 + 15 - 7.5 - 5.625 = 336.875 lb
Tension on L3 = 360 + 30 + 37.5 + 45 + 37.5 + 35.625 = 545.625 lb

Next, we need to calculate is the 120 pounds of cable hanging off the end of the truss, so,

$$\text{Tension on L2} = -\text{Load} \times \frac{D1}{\text{Span}}$$

$$\text{Tension on L2} = -360 \times \frac{10}{20}$$

$$\text{Tension on L2} = -360 \times .5$$

$$\text{Tension on L2} = \text{-180 lb}$$

$$\text{Tension on L3} = \text{Load} - \text{L2}$$
$$\text{Tension on L3} = 360 - (\text{-180})$$
$$\text{Tension on L3} = \text{540 lb}$$

So, adding these numbers to our previous totals, we get:

$$\text{Tension on L1} = 167.5 \,\text{lb}$$
$$\text{Tension on L2} = 336.875 - 180 = 156.875 \,\text{lb}$$
$$\text{Tension on L3} = 545.625 + 540 = 1,085.625 \,\text{lb}$$

Finally, add the 170 pounds of each chain hoist and chain to these points. We now have:

Tension on L1 = 167.5 + 170 = 337.5 lb
Tension on L2 = 156.875 + 170 = 326.875 lb
Tension on L3 = 1,085.625 + 170 = 1,255.625 lb

Problems

1. Calculate the Load on L1 and L2. Dead hung truss is 12 x 12 box and weighs 6 lb per ft. Movers weigh 55 lb each. Lekos weigh 16 lb each. Projectors weigh 75 lb each.

L1   L2

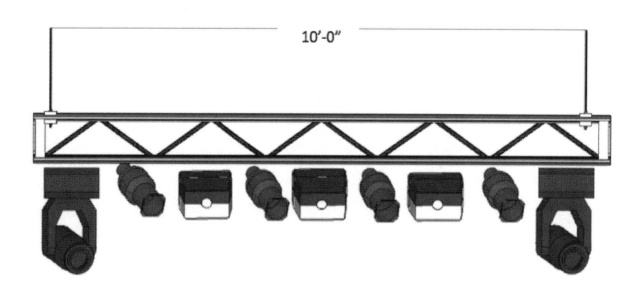

10'-0"

L1= _____ and L2= _____

Unit V: Advanced Rigging

Chapter 16: Chain Hoists and Truss and Lights. Oh my!

2. Calculate the Load on L1 and L2. Dead hung truss is 2 sections of 12" x 12" x 10' box truss. Truss weighs 6 lb per ft. Movers weigh 75 lb each and are positioned 17 ft and 19 ft respectively from point L1. Curtain measures 15; wide x 15' tall and weighs 170 lb.

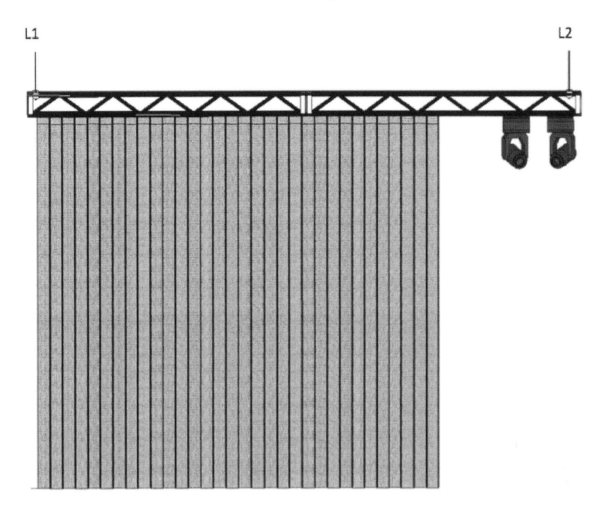

L1= _____ and L2= _____

3. Point Load and Uniform Distributed Load.

Dead hung truss is 2 sections of 12" x 12" x 10' box truss. Truss weighs 6 lb per ft. Curtain measures 20'; wide x 20' tall and weighs 250 lb. Calculate the Loads on L1 and L2 with the curtain in the open position. Calculate the loads on L1 and L2 with the curtain closed.

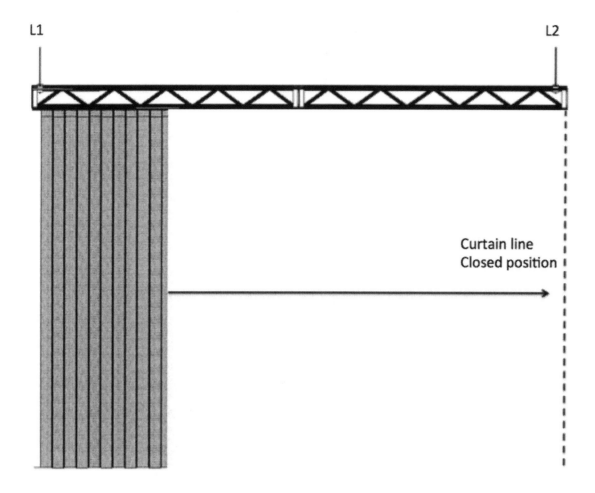

4: Calculate the tensions on L1 and L2 if truss length is 32 ft. Truss weight is 10 lb per ft. Movers weigh 85 lb each.

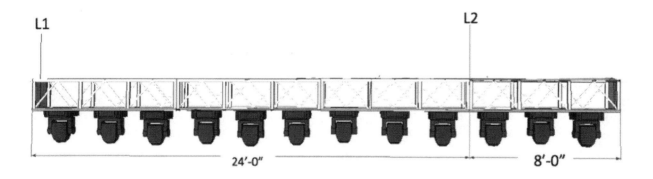

24'-0"   8'-0"

Tension L1 =_____, Tension L2 = _____, Total Load = _____

5. Calculate the tension on L1 and L2. Truss is three sections of 20.5" x 20.5" x 8' box truss. Truss weight is 10 lb per ft. Movers weigh 75 lb each. Lekos weigh 16 lb each. Hoist are 1/2-Ton and weigh 74 lb each. There is 80 ft of chain per hoist. Chain weighs 1/2 lb per ft. Point Load D1 is 18'-0" from the L2 hoist. Point Load D2 is 7'-0" from the L2 hoist.

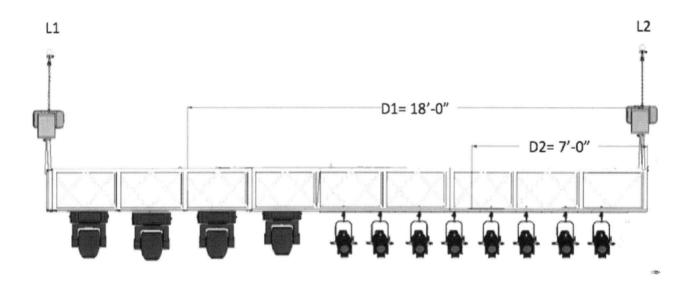

Tension L1 =_____, Tension L2 = _____, Total Load = _____

6. Calculate the tension on L1, L2, and L3. The 40-foot truss is 20.5 x 20.5 and weighs 4.34 lb per ft. Distance between L1 and L2 is 16 ft. Lekos weigh 22 lb each. Movers weigh 75 lb each. There are four electrical cable runs. Cable 1 runs 32 ft onto the truss, cable 2 runs 24 ft onto the truss, cable 3 runs 17 ft onto the truss, and cable 4 runs 8 ft onto the truss. The electrical cable weighs 3 lb per ft. Hoists are 2-Ton and weigh 112 lb each. Hoists have 80 ft of chain. Chain weighs 1 lb per ft. Truss is trimmed at 40 ft.

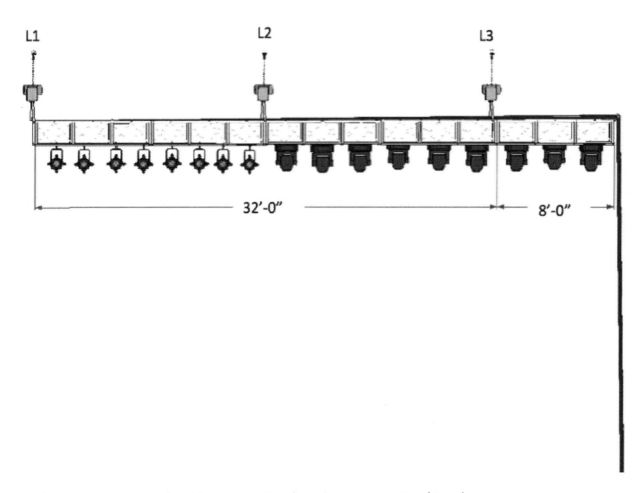

L1   L2   L3

32'-0"   8'-0"

Tension L1 =_____, Tension L2 = _____, Tension L3= _____, Total Load = _____

7. Find the tension on L1, L2, L3, and L4. Truss is 20.5" x 20.5" x 30' and weighs 10 lb per ft. Distance between L1 and L2, L3 and L4 is 7'-6". Distance between L2 and L3 is 10'-0". Cantilevers are 2'-6" ft. Movers weigh 75 lb each. Followspot positions weigh 450 lb including spot operator. Wire rope ladder weight is 50 lb. Hoists are 1-Ton and weigh 114 each. There is 80 ft of chain per hoist. Chain weight is 1 lb per ft. There are two electrical cables: Both cables run 15 ft onto the truss. One cable weighs 3 lb per ft, the other weighs 1 lb per ft. Cable drop is 45 ft.

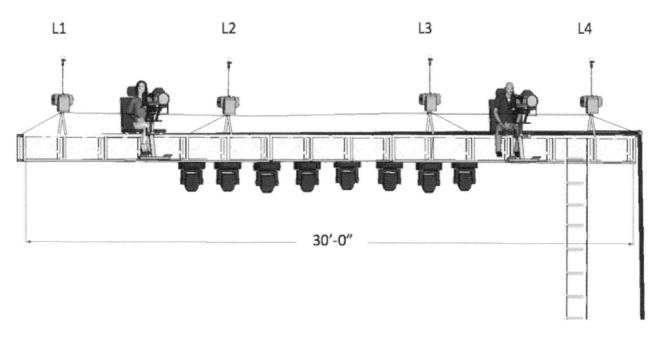

Tension L1 =_____, Tension L2 = _____, Tension L3= _____, Tension L4= _____,

Total Load = _____

8. Calculate the tension on L1 and L2. A 12"x12" x 20' aluminum truss will be dead hung from two points as shown. Truss weight is 7.2 lb per ft. Suspended from the truss will be a six light PAR Bar weighing in at 65 lb, a projector whose weight is 85 lb, and three Vari*lite VL 5 weighing 25 lb each. All electric cables will be suspended from above.

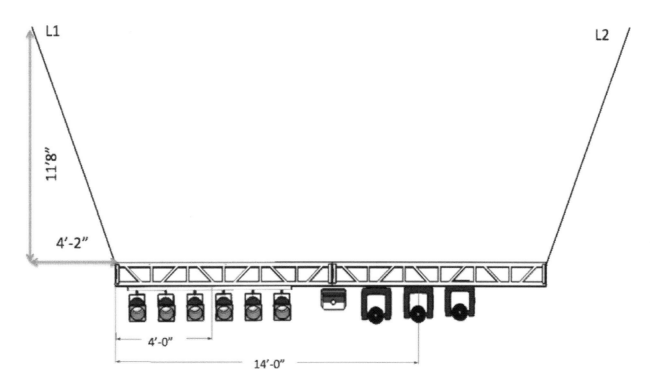

Tension L1 _____, Tension L2_____

Problem 9. A 8500 lb video wall is suspended by six points. The wall measures 50 ft wide x 40 ft tall. Truss is 20.5" x 20.5" x 50' and weights 8.8 lb per ft. Hoist are 2-Ton double reeved and weigh 112 lb each with 80 ft of chain each.

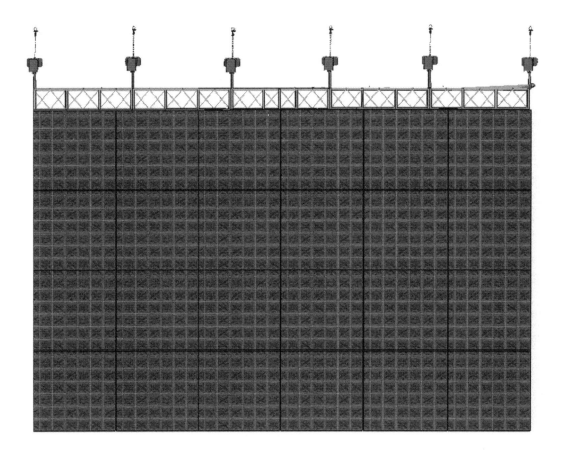

Tension L1 =_____, Tension L2 = _____, Tension L3= _____, Tension L4= _____, Tension L5 =_____,

Tension L6 = _____, Total Load = _____

10. Calculate the tension of L1, L2, L3, L4, and L5. A 20.5" x 30"x 45' ft truss weighs in at 10 lb per ft. Each truss bay is 2.5 ft. Movers are 70 lb each. Mole Fays are 16 lb each, Lekos are 22 lb each. Hoists 1,2,3,4 are 1-Ton and 114 lb each. Hoist 5 is 2-Ton hoist and weighs 112 lb. There is 100 feet of chain per hoist at 1 lb per ft. There are four electrical cable runs. Cable 1 runs 40 ft onto the truss, cable 2 runs 32.5 ft onto the truss, cable 3 runs 22.5 ft onto the truss, and cable 4 runs 12.5 ft onto the truss. Cable drop is 45 ft. Cable weight is 3 lb per ft.

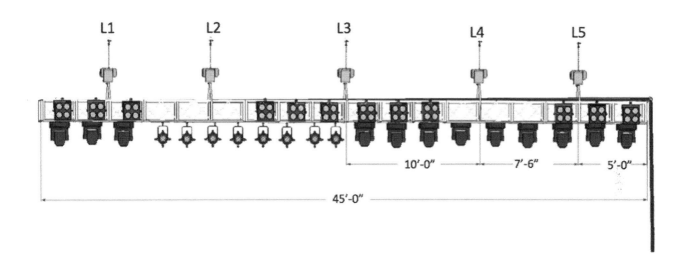

Tension L1 =_____, Tension L2 = _____, Tension L3= _____, Tension L4= _____,

Tension L5= _____, Total Load = _____

11. Calculate the tension on points L1, L2, and L3 on Truss 1. Truss is 20.5"x 20.5" x 32'. Truss weight is 10 lb per ft. There are six PAR Cans weighing 12 lb each spaced on 16" centers. There are three overhead trusses coming in from over stage - Truss A, Truss B, Truss C. The end load from each of these trusses is 843 lb per truss and rest on Truss 1 as shown. Truss A runs 9'-0" onto Truss 2, Truss B runs 20'-8" onto Truss 2, and Truss C runs 29'-0" onto Truss C. There are three 2-Ton hoists each weighing in at 112 lb each. Hoists will have 80 ft of chain weighing 1 lb per ft. There are three electrical cable bundle runs. Cable Bundle 1 runs off Truss A and runs 23'-0" towards L3. Cable Bundle 2 runs 11'-4" towards L3. Cable Bundle 3 runs 3'-0" toward L3. The Cable Bundle drop is 45 ft. Each cable bundle weighs 10 lb per ft.

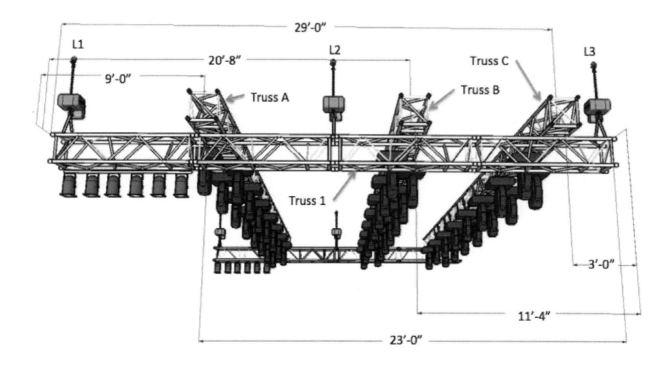

Tension L1 =_____, Tension L2 = _____, Tension L3 = _____, Total Load = _____

12. Overview: Calculate the tensions on each of the eleven rigging point as shown in the diagrams below. The problem will be broken up into three parts as outlined in the following pages.

Problem 11 A. will ask for the tensions on the SR and SR side trusses; Problem 11B will ask for the tensions on the US truss, and Problem 11C will add the video wall. Please note that the US sections of the SR and SL side trusses rest on the US truss and will need to be considered when calculating the loads on the US truss. Problem 11C will add to the US truss a 5000 lb video wall as a *statically determinate structure*. You may need to refer back to Chapter 11.

12 A. Calculate the tension on L1 and L2 for the SR and SL truss sections. L1 supports the center of the truss and L2 supports the downstage most section of the truss. The upstage section (indicated by the arrow) rests on the upstage section. Truss is 20.5" x 20.5" x 32' and consists of four 8 ft sections. Truss weight is 10 lb per ft. Three movers weigh 80 lb each. An 8 ft Par Bar is located on the DS section and weighs 65 lb. Hoists are 1-Ton and weigh 114 lb. Each hoist has 80 ft of chain.

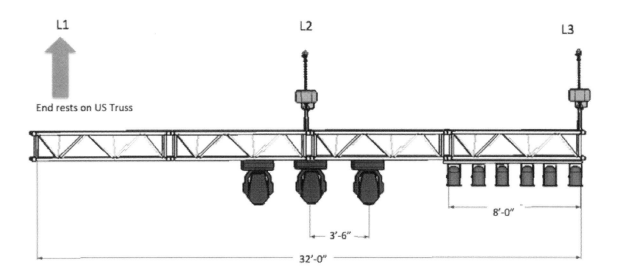

SR and SL Truss

Tension L1 =_____, Tension L2 = _____, Tension L3= _____, Total Load = _____

12 B. The US truss consists of six sections of 20.5 x 20.5 truss and weighs 10 lb per ft. Total truss length is 48 ft. The US ends of the SR and SL truss rest on this truss as shown. Movers weigh 80 lb each. PAR cans weigh 12 lb each. The hoists on this section are 2-Ton and weigh 112 lb each. Chain is 80 ft and weighs 1 lb per ft.

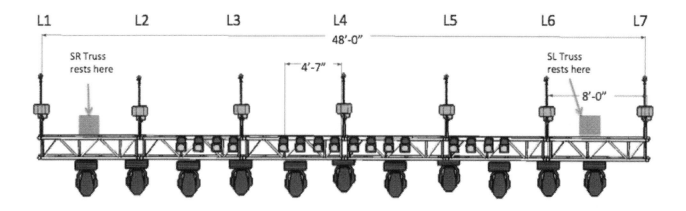

Tension L1 =_____, Tension L2 = _____, Tension L3 = _____, Tension L4 =_____, Tension L5 = _____,

Tension L6 = _____, Tension 7 = _____, Total Load = _____

12 C. Attached to the US Truss is a 5,000 lb video wall. Attachment points are L2, L3, L4, L5 and L6. Please note this is a *Statically Determinate Structure*. You will need to refer to Lesson 11.

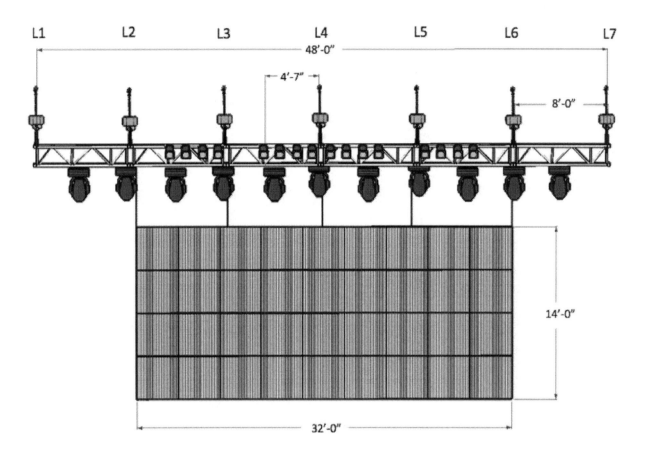

Tension L1 =_____, Tension L2 = _____, Tension L3 = _____, Tension L4 =_____, Tension L5 = _____,

Tension L6 = _____, Tension 7 = _____, Total Load = _____

Answers

1. L1 = 181 lb and L2 = 259 lb, Total Load = 440 lb

2. L1 = 348.7 lb and L2 = 291.5 lb, Total Load = 640.2 lb

3. L1= 250.476 lb, L2= 119.523 lb with the curtain opened. L1= 155 lb, L2= 155 lb with curtain closed.

4. L1 = 390 lb, L2 = 950 lb. Total = 1,340 lb

5. L1 = 496 lb, L2 = 400 lb. Total 896 lb, Total = 896 lb

6. L1 = 321 lb, L 2= 327 lb, L3 = 1676 lb, Total = 2,324 lb

7. L1 = 506 lb, L2 = 785 lb, L3 = 746 lb, L4 = 820 lb, Total = 2,856 lb

8. L1 = 170 lb, L2 = 160 lb

9. L1 = 1,086 lb, L2 = 1,980 lb, L3 = 1,980 lb, L4 = 1,980 lb, L5= 1,980 lb, L6 = 1,086 lb,
    Total = 10,092 lb

10. L1 = 643 lb, L2 = 400 lb, L3 = 634 lb, L4 = 172 lb, L5 = 1,891 lb, Total = 3,739 lb

11. L1 = 710 lb, L2 = 1,770 lb, L3 = 2,740 lb, Total = 5,221 lb

12 A. SR and SL Truss: L1 = 98 lb, L2 = 575 lb, L3 = 340 lb

12 B. US Truss w/o Video Wall: Tension L1 = 321 lb, Tension L2 = 495 lb, Tension L3 = 480 lb,
    Tension L4 = 500 lb, Tension L5 = 480 lb, Tension L6 = 495 lb, Tension 7 = 321 lb,
    Total Load = 3092 lb

12 C. Video Wall = L2 = 490 lb, L3= 1,430 lb, L4 = 1160 lb, L5 = 1,430 lb, L6 = 490 lb

12. Problem Totals, US Truss Totals with Video Wall:
    Tension L1 = 321 lb, Tension L2 = 985 lb, Tension L3 = 1,910 lb, Tension L4 = 1,660 lb,
    Tension L5 = 1,910 lb, Tension L6 = 985 lb, Tension 7 = 321 lb, Total Load = 8,092 lb

Chapter 17:

Ground-Supported Systems

The math for ground-supported systems is very similar to that covered in Chapter 16. However, the hoists are rigging as a 2:1 Mechanical advantage on the towers and therefore only support half of the load at the suspension points. The load on the base of the tower however is 100 percent of the load of the suspension point, plus the weight of the tower (including the hoist and chain). Like the problems in Chapter 16, ground-supported rigs can be simple or complex.

Below is a drawing of the basic parts of a ground-supported truss.

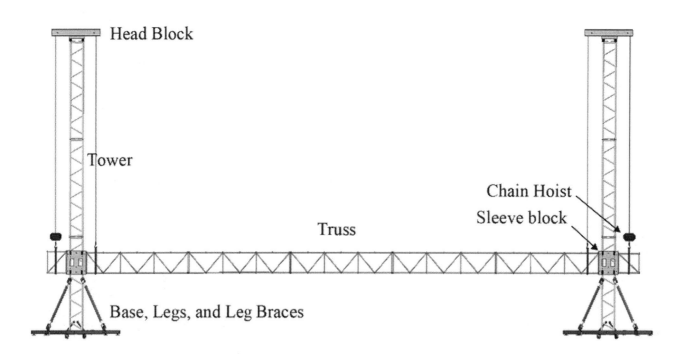

Example: Calculate the load on each of the four towers on the ground-supported rig shown below, including the sleeve block, the hoist and chain. The top of the truss are 30 feet above the floor.

The truss grid is a simple rectangle with three horizontal truss members (Truss 1, Truss 2, and Truss 3) and two vertical members (Truss 4 and Truss 5). The towers are in the corners.

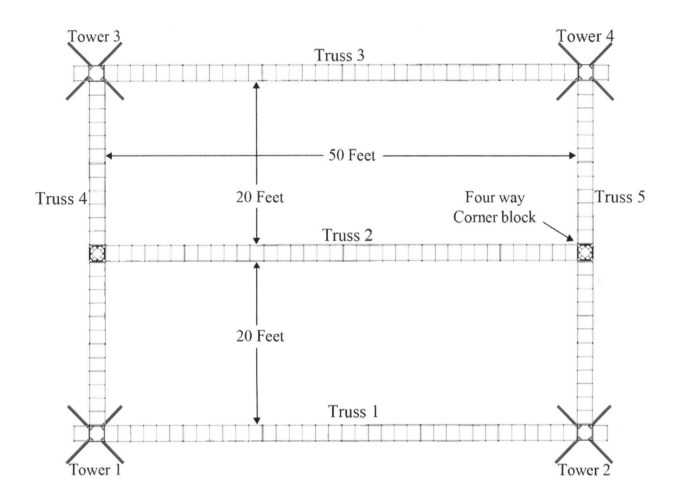

Truss 1, Truss 2, and Truss 3 will have identical loads, except Truss 2 will not have sleeve blocks on the ends. Here is the position of the lights, and the three cable runs.

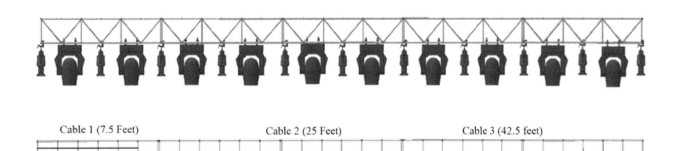

Where:

20.5" x 2.5" Truss = 8.8 lb per foot

Sleeve block = 75 lb

Lekos = 25 lb per instrument

Moving Lights = 75 lb per instruments

Cables = 3 lb per foot per cable

Note: Three cables lay on top of each truss, running from SR: Cable 1 is 7.5 feet long, Cable 2 is 25 feet long, and Cable 3 is 42.5 feet long. The cables will run off the SR end of the truss and drop 30 feet to the ground.

Because the weight of the truss, the moving lights and the Lekos are uniformly distributed across the entire length of the truss, we can total their weights and half of that amount will be distributed to each end of the truss. So,

Truss – 8.8 x 50 = 440 or **220 pounds** per point

Moving lights – 75 x 10 = 750 or **375 pounds** per point

Lekos = 11 x 25 = 275 or **137.5 pounds** per point

This means, at present we have 712.5 pounds of load distributed to SR and SL ends of the truss. Now calculate the distribution of loads for the cables.

We need to calculate four cable runs: the three that run from the SR end of the truss to their various termination points, and the cable drop (three cables that run from the top of the truss to the ground). So,

$$Cable\ Wt = ((wt\!\!/ft \times length) \times (\ \ -(length/2)))/$$

Cable 1 (SR point) = ((3 x 7.5) x (50 – (7.5/2))) / 50

Cable 1 (SR point) = (22.5 x (50 – 3.75)) / 50

Cable 1 (SR point) = (22.5 x 46.25) / 50

Cable 1 (SR point) = (1040.625) / 50

Cable 1 (SR point) = 20.8125 lb

Cable 1 (SL point) = 22.5 – 20.8125

Cable 1 (SL point) = 1.6875 lb

Cable 2 (SR point) = ((3 x 25) x (50 – (25/2))) / 50

Cable 2 (SR point) = (75 x (50 – 12.5)) / 50

Cable 2 (SR point) = (75 x 37.5) / 50

Cable 2 (SR point) = (2812.5) / 50

Cable 2 (SR point) = 56.25 lb

Cable 2 (SL point) = 75 – 56.25

Cable 2 (SL point) = 18.75 lb

Cable 3 (SR point) = ((3 x 42.5) x (50 – (42.5/2))) / 50

Cable 3 (SR point) = (127.5 x (50 – 21.25)) / 50

Cable 3 (SR point) = (127.5 x 28.75) / 50

Cable 3 (SR point) = (3665.625) / 50

Cable 3 (SR point) = 73.125 lb

Cable 3 (SL point) = 127.5 – 73.125

Cable 3 (SL point) = 54.375 lb

Cable Drop (SR) = 3 x 3 x 30

Cable Drop (SR) = 270 lb

So, the total is:

	SR End	SL End
Truss	220.00	220.00
Moving Lights	375.00	375.00
Lekos	137.50	137.50
Cable 1	20.81	1.69
Cable 2	56.25	18.75
Cable 3	73.12	54.38
Cable Drop	270.00	0.00
TOTAL	**1,152.68**	**807.32**

The final step is to add the weight of the sleeve block, the chain hoist, and the chain, as well as half of the weight of Truss 4 and Truss 5 to each tower's load. You get:

	Tower 1	Tower 2	Tower 3	Tower 4
Truss 1	1153.0	807.0	0.0	0.0
Truss 2	610.0	407.5	610.0	407.5
Truss 3	0.0	0.0	1153.0	807.0
Truss 4	194.5	0.0	194.5	0.0
Truss 5	0.0	194.5	0.0	194.5
Sleeve Block	75.0	75.0	75.0	75.0
Chain Hoist	114.0	114.0	114.0	114.0
Chain (70 feet)	70.0	70.0	70.0	70.0
TOTALS	**2,216.5**	**1,468.0**	**2,216.5**	**1,468.0**

Note: These weights do not include the weight of the tower, head block (roller beam), the base, legs or leg braces. A 35-foot tower, with base, will add approximately 500 pounds to each tower. When the tower is placed on the deck of a stage, be certain that the deck can support the weight. Also, guy wires must to used to stabilize each tower.

Problems

1. Calculate the load on each of the two towers on the ground-supported rig shown below, including the sleeve block, the hoist and chain. The top of the truss is 40 feet above the floor. The five large movers weigh 80 lb each. The four small movers weigh 45 lb each. Truss is 20.5" x 20.5" x 32' long and weighs 8.8 lb per ft. The sleeve block is 75 lb each. Each hoists weighs 114 lb each and comes with 80 ft of chain. There are two cable runs. The cables lay on top of the truss, running from SR to SL: Cable 1 is 10 feet long, and Cable 2 is 24 feet long. Cables weigh 3 lb per ft. The cables will run off the SR end of the truss and drop 40 feet to the ground. **Note: Weight totals will not include the weight of the tower, head block (roller beam), the base, legs or leg braces. Guy wires are not included for clarity.**

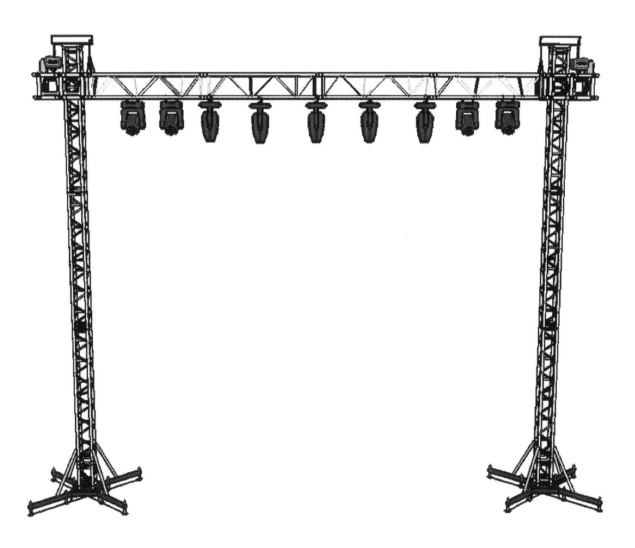

Total: Tower 1 _____   Total: Tower 2 _____

2. Overview:

Calculate the load on all four towers as shown in the three illustrations below. The problem will be broken up into three parts as outlined in the following pages. Problem 2A will ask for the tension on the SR and SL ends of Truss A. Problem 2B will ask for the tension on the SR and SL ends of Truss B. Problem 2C will ask for the tension on the SR and SL ends of Truss C. You will need to keep track of these totals. Problem 2D will add these loads onto the side truss: Truss 1 and Truss 2. **Note: This truss problem does not follow any particular manufacturer's load data.**

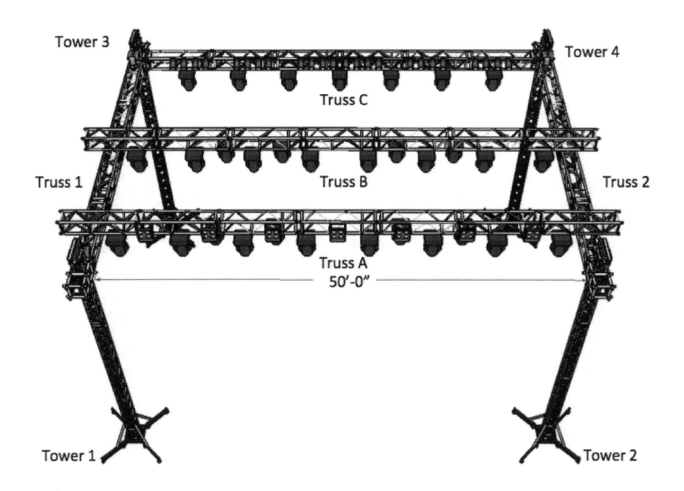

Overview Front Elevation
Overhead View from DS showing the labeling of truss and towers

The towers are 40 ft tall to bottom of truss, and 50' wide - center to center between Towers 1 and 2, and Towers 3 and 4. Truss 1 and 2 are 32'-0" long, center to center between Towers 2 and 4, 1 and 3 respectively.

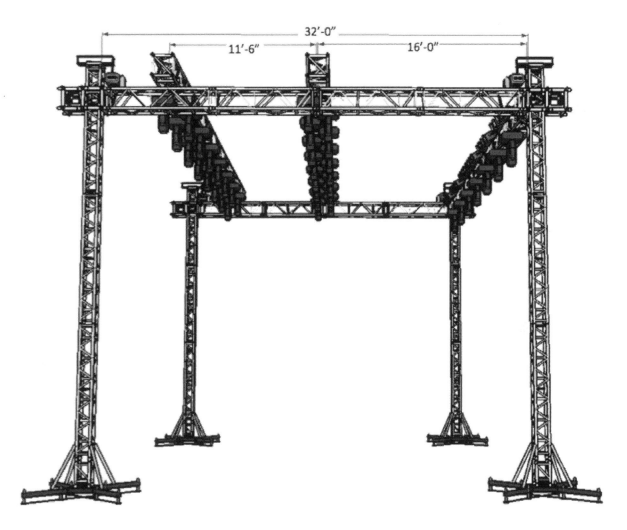

Overview Side Elevation from SL

2 A. Calculate the loads on the SR and SL ends of Truss A. Truss A is a Generic 20.5 x 20.5 x 55' box truss. Weight is 8.8 lb per ft. The ends of Truss A rests on Truss 1 and Truss 2 as shown. The span between Truss 1 and Truss 2 is 50 ft. There are seven Mole Fay audience blinders weighing in at 16 lb each and 12 movers weighing in at 55 lb each. Three cables lay on top of Truss A, running from SR: Cable 1 is 8 ft long, Cable 2 is 25 ft long, and Cable 3 is 40 ft long. The cables will run off the SR end of the truss and follow along Truss 1. Cable weight is 3 lb per ft.

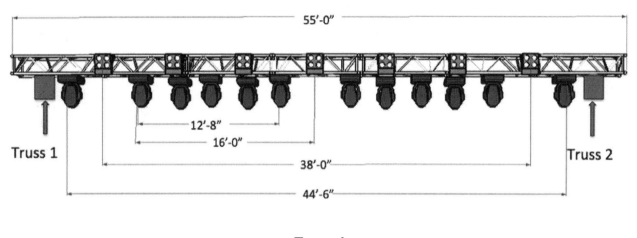

55'-0"

12'-8"

16'-0"

38'-0"

44'-6"

Truss 1

Truss 2

Truss A

SR End_____   SL End _____

2 B. Calculate the loads on the SR and SL ends of Truss B. Truss B is a Generic 20.5x 20.5 x 55' box truss. Weight is 8.8 lb per ft. The ends of Truss B rest on Truss 1 and Truss 2 as shown. The span between Truss 1 and Truss 2 is 50 ft. There are 12 movers weighing in at 55 lb each. Three cables lay on top of Truss B, running from SR: Cable 1 is 8 ft long, Cable 2 is 25 ft long, and Cable 3 is 40 ft long. The cables will run off the SR end of the truss and follow along Truss 1. Cable weight is 3 lb per ft.

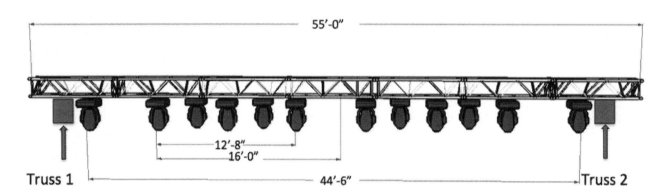

55'-0"

12'-8"
16'-0"

44'-6"

Truss 1

Truss 2

Truss B

SR End_____   SL End _____

2 C. Calculate the loads on the SR and SL ends of Truss C. Truss C is a Generic 20.5" x 20.5" x 50' box truss. Weight is 8.8 lb per ft. The ends of Truss C attach to a sleeve block and then to Truss 1 and Truss 2 as shown. (Note: Sleeve blocks will be counted later with Truss 1 and 2). There are 7 movers weighing in at 55 lb each. In addition, there are 24 PAR Cans weighing 12 lb each. Three cables lay on top of Truss C, running from SR: Cable 1 is 8 ft long, Cable 2 is 25 ft long, and Cable 3 is 40 ft long. The cables will run off the SR end of the truss and follow along Truss 1. Cable weight is 3 lb per ft.

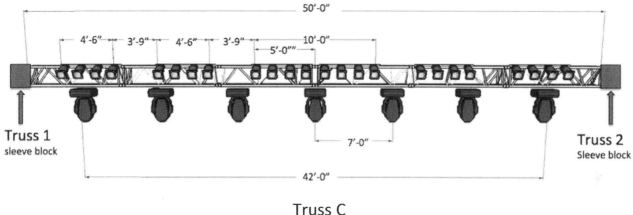

Truss C

SR End_____   SL End _____

2 D. Based on the loads calculated for Truss A, B, and C, calculate the loads on the US and DS ends of Truss 1. Sleeve blocks are 75 lb each. End blocks are 15 lb each. Cable Bundle 1 runs 28.3 ft from Truss A to Truss C. Cable Bundle 2 runs 16 ft from Truss B to Truss C. Cables 1, 2,and 3 will drop 40 ft to ground off Tower 3.

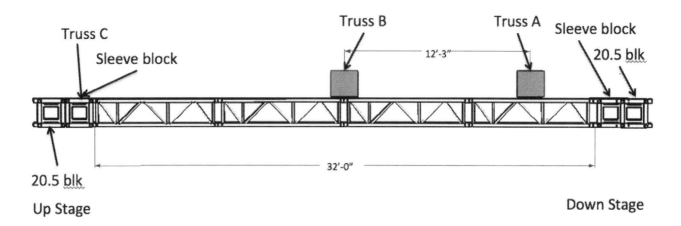

Truss 1

SR End_____   SL End _____

2 E. Based on the loads calculated for Truss A, B, and C, calculate the loads on the US and DS ends of Truss 2. Sleeve blocks are 75 lb each. End blocks are 15 lb each.

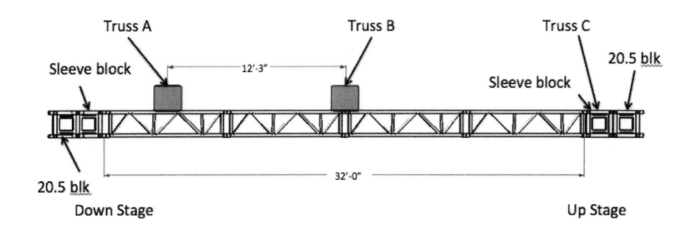

Truss 2

SR End_____   SL End _____

2 F. Calculate the loads for Towers 1, 2, 3, and 4. Hoists are 2T and weigh 112 lb. Each hoist has 80 ft of chain weighing 1 lb per ft.

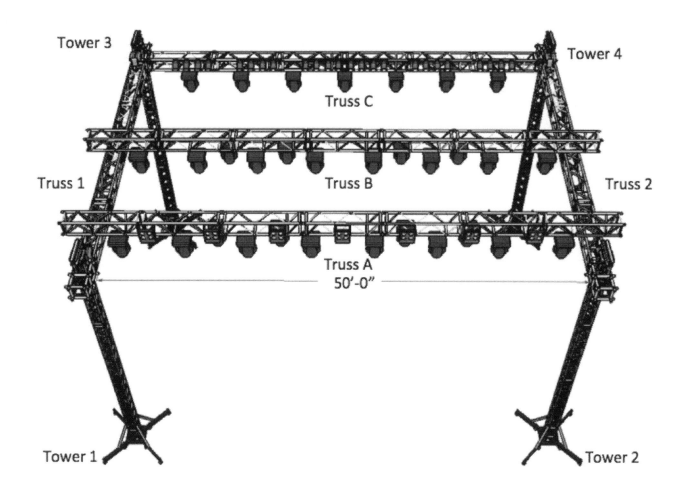

	Tower 1	Tower 2	Tower 3	Tower 4
Truss 1	_____		_____	
Truss 2		_____		_____
Chain Hoist	_____	_____	_____	_____
Chain (80 feet)	_____	_____	_____	_____
TOTALS	_____	_____	_____	_____

Note: These weights do not include the weight of the tower, head block (roller beam), the base, legs or leg braces. A 35-foot tower, with base, will add approximately 500 pounds to each tower. When the tower is placed on the deck of a stage, be certain that the deck can support the weight. Also, guy wires must to used to stabilize each tower. This truss problem does not follow any particular manufacturer's load data. Truss manufacturer's load data charts MUST be consulted at all times.

3 A and 3 B. Overview:

Based on the loads calculated for Problem 2, calculate the loads on the SR and SL Speaker Array Towers. Towers are 40 ft from bottom of truss to floor. Speakers and arrays are 2,000 lb each. These loads will need to be added to the loads on Towers 1 and 2.

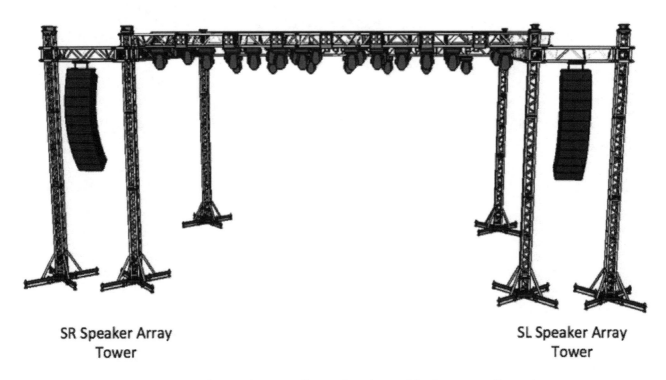

SR Speaker Array
Tower

SL Speaker Array
Tower

Truss is Generic 20.5 x 20.5 x 8'. Weight is 8.8 lb per ft. Sleeve blocks are 75 lb each. Hoists are 112 lb on each tower. Chain is 80 ft. Speaker Cable not shown.

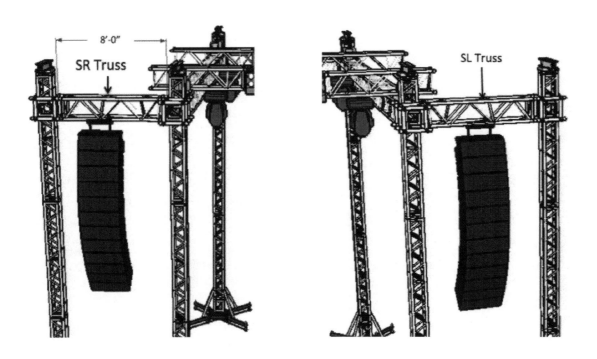

SR Speaker Tower Truss

SR Speaker Truss End   SL Speaker Truss End (Tower 1)

Totals   _____   _____

SL Speaker Tower Truss

SR Speaker Truss End   SL Speaker Truss End (Tower 2)

Totals   _____   _____

Answers

1.

	SR End	**SL End**
Truss	141.00	141.00
Moving Lights	290.00	290.00
Cable 1	25.00	5.00
Cable 2	45.00	27.00
Cable Drop	240.00	0.00
TRUSS TOTAL	**741.00 lb**	**463.00 lb**
Sleeve Block	75	75
Chain Hoist	114	114
80' Chain	80	80
TOWER TOTAL	**269 lb**	**269 lb**
TOTALS	Tower 1 = 1,010 lb	Tower 2 = 732 lb

2 A. Truss A

	SR End	**SL End**
Truss	242 lb	242 lb
Moving Lights	330 lb	330 lb
Mole Fays	56 lb	56 lb
Cable 1	22 lb	2 lb
Cable 2	58 lb	17 lb
Cable 3	76 lb	44 lb
TOTAL	**778 lb**	**697 lb**

2 B. Truss B

	SR End		SL End
Truss	242 lb		242 lb
Moving Lights	330 lb		330 lb
Cable 1	22 lb		2 lb
Cable 2	56 lb		19 lb
Cable 3	72 lb		48 lb
TOTAL	**722 lb**		**641 lb**

2 C. Truss C

	SR End		SL End
Truss	220 lb		242 lb
Moving Lights	192.5 lb		192.5 lb
PAR Cans	144 lb		144 lb
Cable 1	22 lb		2 lb
Cable 2	56 lb		19 lb
Cable 3	72 lb		48 lb
TOTAL	**706.5 lb**		**625.5 lb**

2 D. Truss 1

	US End		DS End
Truss	141 lb		141 lb
20.5 end block	15 lb		15 lb
Sleeve Blocks	75 lb		75 lb
Truss A	90 lb		688 lb
Truss B	361 lb		361 lb
Truss C	707 lb		0 lb
Cable 1	141 lb		111 lb
Cable 2	108 lb		36 lb
Cable 3	0 lb		0 lb
Cable Drop	1,080 lb		0 lb
TOTAL	**2,717 lb**		**1,427 lb**

2 E.   Truss 2

	DS End	**US End**
Truss	141 lb	141 lb
20.5 end block	15 lb	15 lb
Sleeve Blocks	75 lb	75 lb
Truss A	616 lb	81 lb
Truss B	321 lb	321 lb
Truss C	0 lb	626 lb
TOTAL	**1,168 lb**	**1,259 lb**

2 F.

	Tower 1	Tower 2	Tower 3	Tower 4
Truss 1	1,427.0 lb		2,717.0 lb	
Truss 2		1,168 lb		1,259.0 lb
Chain Hoist	112.0 lb	112.0 lb	112.0 lb	112.0 lb
Chain (80 feet)	80.0 lb	80.0 lb	80.0 lb	80.0 lb
TOTALS	**1,619.0 lb**	**1,360.0 lb**	**2,909 lb**	**1,4651.0 lb**

3 A and 3 B.

SR Speaker Tower Truss

SR Truss End	1,035 lb	SL Truss End	1,035 lb
Tower 1	0 lb		1,619 lb
Sleeve Block	75 lb		0 lb
Hoist	112 lb		0 lb
Chain Weight	80 lb		0 lb
Totals	1,302 lb		2,654 lb

SL Speaker Tower Truss

SR Truss End	1,035 lb	SL Truss End	1,035 lb
Tower 2	1,360 lb		0 lb
Sleeve Block	0 lb		75 lb
Hoist	0 lb		112 lb
Chain Weight	0 lb		80 lb
Totals	2,395 lb		1,302 lb

Chapter 18:
Effective Length of Hitch

A quick and simple formula for calculating the ELOH measurement is:

ELOH = ((Length of sling + (1.5 × $shackle\ length$)) − (Height of beam + width of beam)) / 2

Let's test this on a 12" x 9" beam and a 5-foot basket.

ELOH = ((60 + (1.5 × 2.375) − (12+9)) / 2

ELOH = ((60 + 3.5625) − 21) / 2

ELOH = (63.5625 − 21) / 2

ELOH = 42.5625 / 2

ELOH = 21.28125 inches

Problems

1. What is the ELOH for an 18" x 18" beam and a 10-foot steel basket and a 5/8 in shackle?

2. What is the ELOH for a 22" x 18" beam and a 10-foot steel basket and a 5/8 in shackle?

3. What is the ELOH for a 16" x 16" beam and a 5-foot steel basket and a 5/8 in shackle?

4. What is the ELOH for a 30" x 12" beam and a 10-foot steel basket and a 5/8 in shackle?

5. What is the ELOH for a 12" x 12" beam and a 5-foot steel basket with a ¾ in shackle?

6. What is the ELOH for a 17" x 19" beam and a 5 and a 2-foot steel basket with a ¾ in shackle?

7. What is the ELOH for a 25" x 18" beam and a 10 and a 5-foot steel basket with a ¾ in shackle?

8. What is the ELOH for a 20" x 15" beam and a 10-foot steel basket with a 5/8 in shackle?

9. What is the ELOH for a 28" x 18" beam and a 10 and a 5-foot steel basket with a ¾ in shackle?

10. What is the ELOH for a 10" x 10" beam and a 5-foot steel basket and a 5/8 in shackle?

11. What is the ELOH for a 14" x 10" beam and a 5-foot steel basket and a 5/8 in shackle?

12. What is the ELOH for a 13" x 8" beam and a 5-foot steel basket and a ¾ in shackle?

13. What is the ELOH for an 11.4" x 8.2" beam and a 5-foot steel basket and a ¾ in shackle?

14. What is the ELOH for a 15.4" x 11.8" beam and a 5 and a 2.5-foot steel basket and a 5/8 in shackle?

15. What is the ELOH for a 33" x 28.7" beam and a 10 and a 5-foot steel basket and a 5/8 in shackle?

16. What is the ELOH for a 39.3" x 45" beam and a 20-foot steel basket and a ¾ in shackle?

17. What is the ELOH for a 45.2" x 38.2" beam and a 20-foot steel basket and a ¾ in shackle?

18. What is the ELOH for a 17" x 13.3" beam and a 10 and a 5-foot steel basket and a ¾ in shackle?

19. What is the ELOH for a 40" x 32.5" beam and a 10-foot steel basket and a 5/8 in shackle?

20. What is the ELOH for a 22.3" x 18" beam and a 20-foot steel basket and a ¾ in shackle?

Answers

1. 43.78125 inches

2. 41.78125 inches

3. 15.78125 inches

4. 40.78125 inches

5. 20.25 inches

6. 29.25 inches

7. 73.75 inches

8. 44.28125 inches

9. 72.25 inches

10. 21.78125 inches

11. 19.78125 inches

12. 21.75 inches

13. 22.45 inches

14. 35.55625 inches

15. 63.30625 inches

16. 80.1 inches

17. 80.55 inches

18. 80.1 inches

19. 25.53125 inches

20. 102.1 inches

Chapter 19:

Two-Point Bridles in an Arena

The problems in this chapter will ask you to make up bridle legs based on the ELOH (Chapter 18) and Length of Bridle Legs (Chapter 5). Remember, the Bridle Point needs to be placed between the minimum and maximum distance above the deck. Bridle angles MUST not exceed 120 degrees (90 degrees preferred).

Example: The Bridle Point is 10 feet from one I-beam and 15 feet from the second I-beam. The I-beams are 80 feet above the deck. The bridle point needs to be a minimum height of 40 feet above the deck, and a maximum height of the bridle point is 65 feet above the deck. The Bridle Point can be anywhere along the 25-foot long space between these points.

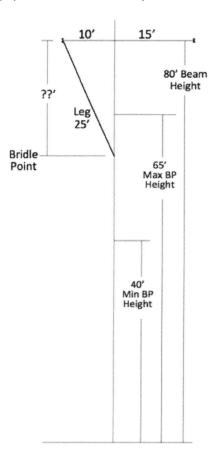

The following bridle lengths will work: 20', 25', 30', 35', and 40 feet. In this example, we have choose an approximate bridle length of 25 feet (which will be made from a 20-foot and a 5-foot sling (joined by a shackle). Note: If only one sling is needed to make the desired length, no shackles will need to be added. But, if three slings are needed to create the desired length, then two shackles will be needed in order to attach the three slings together. So,

Leg 1 = 25 (the sling) + 1.781995096 (the ELOH in feet) + 0.197916667 (the length of one shackle in feet)

Leg 1 = 26.97991176

or

Leg 1 = 27 feet

Next, we need to calculate the third leg of the triangle (the Vertical distance from the apex to the beam) using a variation of the Pythagorean Theorem:

$$V = \sqrt{(Leg \times Leg) - (H \times H)}$$

So, plugging in the numbers, we get…

$$V = \sqrt{(27 \times 27) - (10 \times 10)}$$

$$V = \sqrt{729 - 100}$$

$$V = \sqrt{629}$$

$$V = 25.08$$

or

V = 25 feet

Now, we need to find the TOTAL length of the <u>other</u> bridle leg (Leg 2). We use the Pythagorean Theorem with the Horizontal distance of 15 feet and the Vertical distance is 25.26 feet to get:

$$Leg = \sqrt{(15 \times 15) + (25.08 \times 25.08)}$$

$$Leg = \sqrt{225 + 629.0064}$$

$$Leg = \sqrt{854.0064}$$

Leg = 29.223 feet

Now we need to figure-out how to make this leg.

First, we subtract the ELOH for the basket. So,

L2 = 29.223 - 1.781995096

L2 = 27.4410049

Next, we look at what steel and hardware will make this length.

A 20' steel + 5' steel + 0.1979 shackle = 25.1979 feet.

27.4410049 - 25.1979 = 2.2431049 feet needed to finish leg.

The remaining length can be made with a 2-foot "dog bone" plus one shackle or 8 Links of 3.174" STAC.

So, to make this bridle, we need:

Leg 1: One 5 foot with 2 shackle for basket, one 20 foot sling, one 5 foot sling and two shackles (one for the leg and the other for the apex)

Leg 2: One 5 foot with 2 shackle for basket, one 20 foot sling, one 5 foot sling and two shackles (one of the leg and one for the STAC), and 8 Links of STAC chain.

Note: Apex to floor = 54.74 feet

Problems

The following problems will ask you to make up the desired length legs using the following: Steel: 2', 2.5', 5', 10', 20,' 30', and 50' lengths, 3-ft and 5-ft Deck Chain, Shackles: 5/8" (2.375"). Deck Chain Links = 3.174". Basket length is stated as part of the problem and will use the accurate method of calculating the ELOH as described in Chapter 18.

1. Overview:
The I Beams in an arena are 25" x 20" and spaced 30 feet apart. Basket will be 10 feet long. The heights of the beams to the arena floor are 100 feet. The bridle point will be a maximum distance of

73 feet and minimum distance of 65 ft. below the I beams. The apex will be 17'-6" to the left of Beam B. Approximate base length of Leg 1 (+ELOH and shackles) will be 30 feet. The Bridle Point can be anywhere along between the 65' and 80' minimum and maximum distance. Steel will be 3/8" with 5/8" shackles.

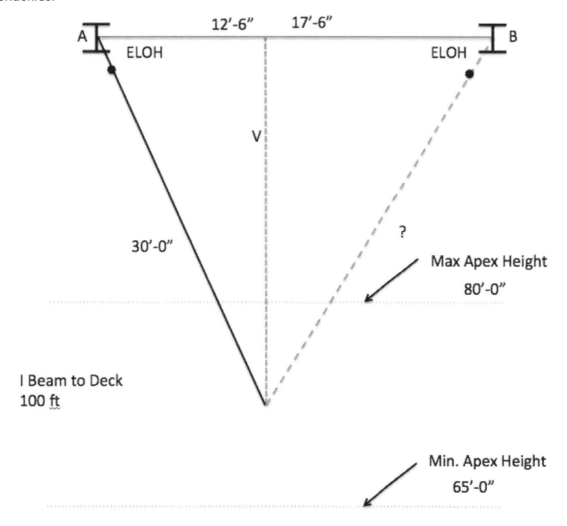

1 A. Calculate the ELOH of the 10 ft Basket for the two 25 x 20" I beams (including shackles). Basket will be a straight 10 ft.

1 B. Calculate the total length of Bridle Leg 1 including basket return (ELOH) and shackles. Approximate base length of the steel is 30'-0".

1 C. Calculate the vertical distance using a variation of the Pythagorean Theorem for Legs 1 and 2.

1 D. Find the total length of the hypotenuse for Leg 2.

1 E. Calculate the distance needed to complete Leg 2.

1 F. Make up the steel and STAC chain (and/or dog bone) necessary for Leg 2

1 G. What is the distance from the apex to the floor?

2. Overview:

The I Beams in an arena are 24" x 18" and spaced 23'-6" apart. Basket will be 10 feet. The heights of the beams to the arena floor are 85 feet. The bridle point will be a maximum distance of 73 feet and minimum distance of 65 feet. below the I beams. The Bridle Point can be anywhere along the 65' and 73' minimum and maximum distance. The apex will be 13.417 feet left of Beam B. The approximate base length of Leg 1 (including the ELOH and shackles) will be 17'-6". Steel will be 3/8" with 5/8" shackles.

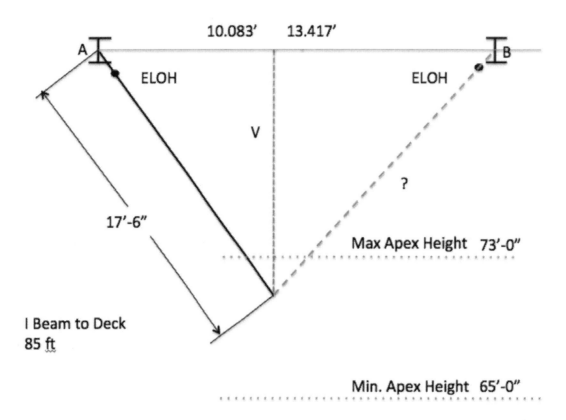

2 A. Calculate the ELOH of the basket for the two 24"x 18" I beams including shackles. Basket will be a straight 10 ft.

2 B. Calculate the total length of Bridle Leg 1 including basket return (ELOH) and shackles. Approximate base length of the steel is 17'-6".

2 C. Calculate the Vertical distance using a variation of the Pythagorean Theorem for Legs 1 and 2.

2 D. Find the total length of the hypotenuse for Leg 2.

2 E. Calculate the distance needed to complete Leg 2.

2 F. Make up the steel and STAC chain (and/or dog bone) necessary for Leg 2

2 G. What is the distance from the Apex to the Floor?

3. Overview:

The I Beams in a convention center are 15" x 10" and spaced 16.0833 feet apart. Basket will be 5 feet. The heights of the beams to the arena floor are 40 feet. There is little headroom so the bridle point should be between 30 feet and 35 feet above the deck. The apex will be 9.0833 feet to the left of Beam B. The approximate base length of Leg 1 (including the ELOH and shackles) will be 7.5'.

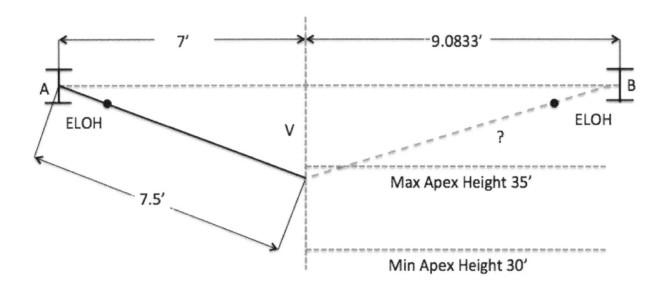

3 A. Calculate the ELOH of the basket for the two 15"x 10" I beams including shackles. Basket will be a straight 5 ft.

3 B. Calculate the total length of Bridle Leg 1 including basket return (ELOH) and shackles. Approximate base length of the steel is 7.5'.

3 C. Calculate the Vertical distance using a variation of the Pythagorean Theorem for Legs 1 and 2.

3 D. Find the total length of the hypotenuse for Leg 2.

3 E. Calculate the distance needed to complete Leg 2.

3 F. Make up the steel and STAC chain (and/or dog bone) necessary for Leg 2

3 G. Calculate the bridle angle making sure the angle does NOT exceed 120 degrees.

3 H. What is the distance from the Apex to the Floor?

4. Overview:

The I Beams in an arena are 12" x 18" and spaced 18 ft apart. Baskets will be 5 ft. The heights of the beams to the arena floor are 80 ft for the Beam A and 82 ft for Beam B. The Bridle Point will be a maximum distance of 69 ft and a minimum distance of 60 ft . The Bridle Point can be anywhere along the 69' and 60' minimum and maximum distance. The apex will be 9.750 to the left of Beam B. The approximate base length of Leg 1 (+ELOH and shackles) will be 15'-0".

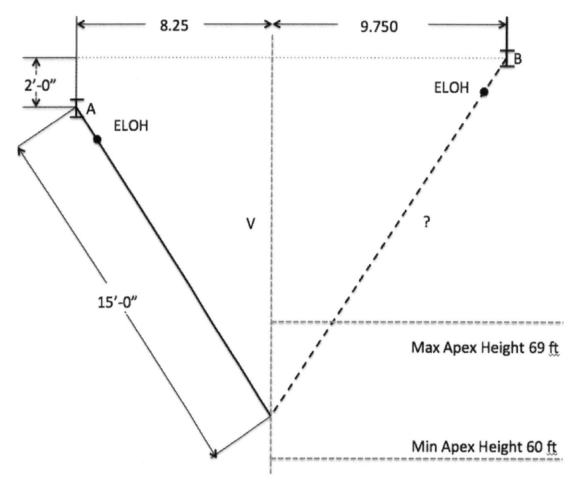

4 A. Calculate the ELOH of the basket for the two 12"x 18" I-beams including shackles. Basket will be a straight 5-foot.

4 B. Calculate the total length of Bridle Leg 1 including basket return (ELOH) and shackles. Approximate base length of the steel is 15'-0".

4 C. Calculate the Vertical distance using a variation of the Pythagorean Theorem for Leg 1 and Leg 2.

4 D. Find the total length of the hypotenuse for Leg 2.

4 E. Calculate the distance needed to complete Leg 2.

4 F. Make up the steel and STAC chain (and/or dog bone) necessary for Leg 2

4 G. What is the distance from the Apex to the Floor from the SL I-Beam?

5. Overview:

The I Beams in an arena are 24" x 20" and spaced 11 feet apart. Basket will be a Split 7.5-foot. The heights of the beams to the arena floor are 53.583 feet for Beam A and 55 feet for Beam B. The bridle point will be a maximum distance of 50 feet and a minimum distance of 46 feet. The Bridle Point can be anywhere along the 40-foot to 50-foot minimum and maximum distance. The apex will be 7.5833 feet to the left of Beam B. The approximate base length of Leg 1 (including the ELOH and shackles) will be 7.5'.

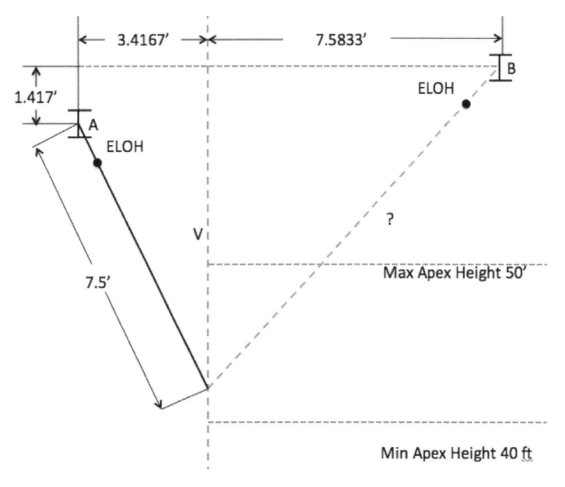

5 A. Calculate the ELOH of the basket for the two 24"x 20" I beams including shackles. Basket is a split 7.5 ft.

5 B. Calculate the total length of Bridle Leg 1 including basket return (ELOH) and shackles. Approximate base length of the steel is 7.5'.

5 C. Calculate the Vertical distance using a variation of the Pythagorean Theorem for Leg 1 and Leg 2.

5 D. Find the total length of the hypotenuse for Leg 2.

5 E. Calculate the distance needed to complete Leg 2.

5 F. Make up the steel and STAC chain (and/or dog bone) necessary for Leg 2.

6. Overview:

The I-Beams in an arena are 28" x 25" and spaced 11'-0" feet apart. Basket will be a split 15-foot. The heights of the beams to the arena floor are 90 feet. The bridle point will be a maximum distance of 85 feet and minimum distance of 70 feet below the I-beams. The apex will be 8'-0" to the left of Beam B. The approximate base length of Leg 1 (including the ELOH and shackles) will be 10'-0". Steel will be 3/8" with 5/8" shackles. There is an 1800 lb load on the apex.

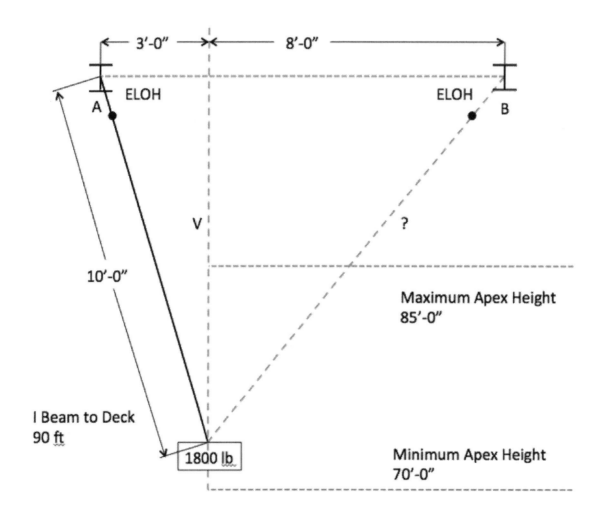

6 A. Calculate the ELOH of the basket for the two 28"x 25" I beams including shackles. Basket is a split 15-foot.

6 B. Calculate the total length of Bridle Leg 1 including basket return (ELOH) and shackles. Approximate base length of the steel is 10'-0".

6 C. Calculate the Vertical distance using a variation of the Pythagorean Theorem for Leg 1 and Leg 2.

6 D. Find the total length of the hypotenuse for Leg 2.

6 E. Calculate the distance needed to complete Leg 2.

6 F. Make up the steel and STAC chain (and/or dog bone) necessary for Leg 2

6 G. Calculate the tension on Legs 1 and 2 if the load on the apex is 1800 lb.

7. Overview:

The I-Beams in an arena are 32" x 26" and spaced 20 feet apart. Basket will be a Split 15-foot. The heights of the beams to the arena floor are 100 feet for Beam A and 99 feet for Beam B. The bridle point will be a maximum distance of 80 feet and a minimum distance of 65 feet to the floor. The apex will be 12.5 feet from Beam B. The approximate base length of Leg 1 (including the ELOH and shackles) will be 25'-0".

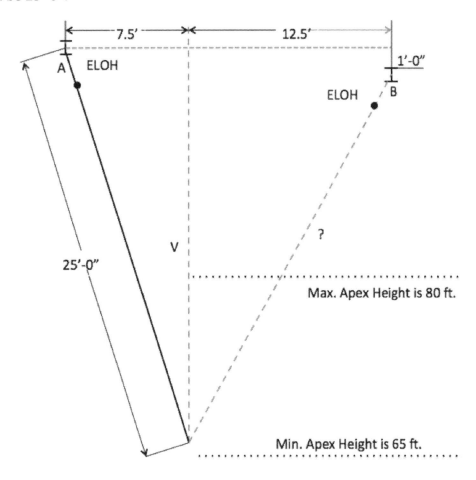

7 A. Calculate the ELOH of the basket for the two 32"x 26" I beams including shackles. Basket is a split 15-foot.

7 B. Calculate the total length of Bridle Leg 1 including basket return (ELOH) and shackles. Approximate base length of the steel is 25'-0".

7 C. Calculate the Vertical distance using a variation of the Pythagorean Theorem for Leg 1 and Leg 2.

7 D. Find the total length of the hypotenuse for Leg 2.

7 E. Calculate the distance needed to complete Leg 2.

7 F. Make up the steel and STAC chain (and/or dog bone) necessary for Leg 2.

8. Overview:

The I Beams in an arena are 20" x 16" and spaced 22 feet apart. Basket will be a Split 7.5-foot. The heights of the beams to the arena floor are 90 feet for Beam A and 85.833 feet for Beam B. The bridle point will be a maximum distance of 80 feet from Beam A to the floor and a minimum distance of 65 feet to the floor. The Bridle Point can be anywhere along the 65-foot to 80 foot minimum and maximum distance. The apex will be 14.5 feet from Beam B. The approximate base length of Leg 1 (including the ELOH and shackles) will be 12'-6".

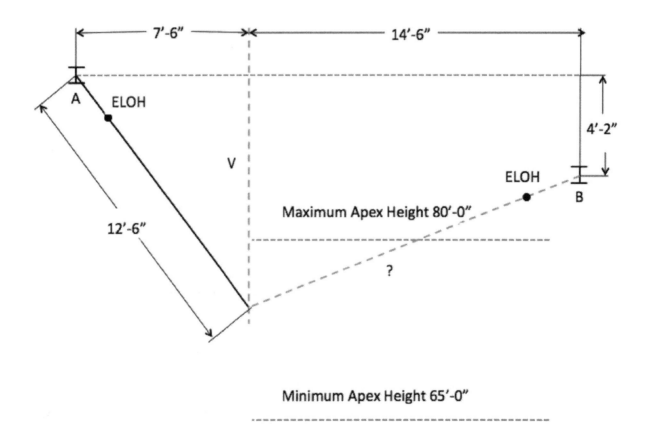

8 A. Calculate the ELOH of the basket for the two 20"x 16" I beams including shackles. Basket is a split 7.5 ft.

8 B. Calculate the total length of Bridle Leg 1 including basket return (ELOH) and shackles. Approximate base length of the steel is 12'-6".

8 C. Calculate the Vertical distance using a variation of the Pythagorean Theorem for Leg 1 and Leg 2.

8 D. Find the total length of the hypotenuse for Leg 2.

8 E. Calculate the distance needed to complete Leg 2.

8 F. Make up the steel and STAC chain (and/or dog bone) necessary for Leg 2.

8 G. Calculate the bridle angle making sure the angle does NOT exceed 120 degrees.

Answers

1 A. 3.2734 feet

1 B. 33.67 feet including 2 shackles for the 20-foot and 10-foot steel

1 C. 31.26 feet

1 D. 35.83 feet

1 E. ELOH 32.555 − 30.397 = 2.16 feet is needed to complete Leg 2.

1 F. Hardware needed: Leg 2 = 20-foot steel + 10-foot steel + 0.1983 shackle + 0.1983 shackle = 30.397 ft.   Add 8 Links of STAC (3.174") = 2.116 feet

1 G. 68.73 feet

2 A. 3.3984 feet

2 B. 21.59 feet including 3 shackles for the 10-foot, 5-foot and 2.5-foot steel

2 C. 19.09 feet

2 D. 23.34 feet

2 E. ELOH 19.939 − 18.095 = 1.84 feet is needed to complete Leg 2

2 F. Answer: Hardware needed: Leg 2= 10-foot steel + 5-foot steel + 2.5" steel + 0.1983 shackle + 0.1983 shackle + 0.1983 shackle = 18.095 feet. 7 Links of STAC (3.174") = 1.852 feet

2 G. 65.91 feet

3 A. 1.6068 feet

3 B. 9.50 feet including 2 shackle for the 5-foot steel and 2.5-foot steel

3 C. 6.43 feet

3 D. 11.13 feet

3 E. ELOH 9.521 feet – 7.897 feet = 1.62 feet is needed to complete Leg 2

3 F. Hardware needed: Leg 2= 5-foot steel + 2.5-foot steel + 0.1983 shackle + 0.1983 shackle = 7.897 feet. 6 Links of STAC (3.174") = 1.587 feet

3 G. 102.12 degrees

3 H. 33.57 feet

4 A. 1.3984 feet

4 B. 16.80 feet including 2 shackles for the 10-foot steel, 5-foot steel

4 C. 14.63 feet for Leg 1, 16.63 feet for Leg 2

4 D. 19.28 feet

4 E. ELOH 17.879 – 15.397 = 2.48 feet is needed to complete Leg 2

4 F. Hardware needed: Leg 2 = 10-foot steel + 5-foot steel + 0.1983 shackle + 0.1983 shackle = 15.397 ft. 9 Links of STAC (3.174") = 2.381 feet

4 G. 63.37 feet

5 A. 2.2630 feet

5 B. 10.16 feet including 2 shackles for the 5-foot and 2.5-foot steel

5 C. 9.75 feet for Leg 1. 10.98 feet for Leg 2

5 D. 13.35 feet

5 E. ELOH 11.085 – 10.198 = .89 feet is needed to complete Leg 2

5 F. Hardware needed: Leg 2 = 10-feet steel + 0.1983 shackle = 10.198 feet + 3 Links of STAC (3.174") = 0.794 feet

6 A. 5.6380 feet

6 B. 15.84 feet including 1 shackle for apex

6 C. 15. 55 feet for Legs 1 and 2

6 D. 17.49 feet

6 E. ELOH 11.849 − 10.198 = 1.65 feet is needed to complete Leg 2.

6 F. Hardware needed: Leg 2 = 10-foot steel + 0.1983 shackle = 10.198 ft. 6 Links of STAC (3.174") = 1.587 feet

6 G. Tension Leg 1= 1333.23 lb, Tension Leg 2= 552.07

7 A. 5.4297 feet

7 B. 30.83 feet including 1 shackle for apex

7 C. 29.70 feet for Leg 1 and 28.90 feet for Leg 2

7 D. 31.49 feet

7 E. ELOH 26.058 − 25.357 = 0.66 feet is needed to complete Leg

7 F. Hardware needed: Leg 2 = 20-foot steel, 5-foot steel, + 0.1983 shackle + 0.1983 shackle = 25.397 feet + 2 Links of STAC (3.174") = 0.529 feet

8 A. 2.5964 feet

8 B. 15.49 feet including 2 shackle for the 10-foot and 5-foot steel

8 C. 13.56 feet for Leg 1 and 9.39 feet for Leg 2

8 D. 17.27 feet

8 E. ELOH 14.679 − 12.879 = 1.78 feet is needed to complete Leg 2

8 F. Hardware needed: Leg 2 = 10-foot steel + 2.5 foot steel + 0.1983 shackle + 0.1983 shackle = 12.879 feet + 7 Links of STAC = 1.852 feet

8 G. 86.02 degrees

Chapter 20:
Math Tools of the Trade

This Chapter will ask you to solve problems using the three Excel workbooks: The Bridle Calculator, the Truss Load Workbook, and Bridle Calculator Pro, that you can download for free from: www.SpringKnollPress.com/RiggingMath/downloads. If you enter the provided information correctly, you should get the answers listed at the end of this chapter.

The Bridle Calculator

For the following problems, find the Bridle Lengths of Legs 1 and Legs 2 using the Bridle Calculator. The inside length of deck chain will be 3.125 inches. Note: Be sure to compare the final bridle point to floor measurement with the minimum and maximum distances. Answer should fall within this range.

Problems

1. The height of Beam 1 is 12 inches, the width is 9 inches.
   The height of Beam 2 is 12 inches, the width is 9 inches.
   Height above deck is: 80 feet.
   Horizontal Distance from Beam 1 is: 10 feet, Horizontal Distance from Beam 2 is: 15 feet.
   Minimum Bridle Point Height will be 40 feet; Maximum Bridle Point Length is 67 feet.
   Baskets will be made from 10 foot steel.
   Basic Bridle Length will be 25 feet.

2. The height of Beam 1 is 18 inches, the width is 20 inches.
   The height of Beam 2 is 18 inches, the width is 20 inches.
   Height above deck is: 100 feet.
   Horizontal Distance from Beam 1 is: 9 feet, Horizontal Distance from Beam 2 is: 16 feet.
   Minimum Bridle Point Height will be 65 feet; Maximum Bridle Point Length is 80 feet.
   Baskets will be made from 15 foot split.
   Basic Bridle Length will be 25 feet.

3. The height of Beam 1 is 32 inches, the width is 26 inches.

    The height of Beam 2 is 32 inches, the width is 26 inches.

    Height above deck is: 102 feet.

    Horizontal Distance from Beam 1 is: 5 feet, Horizontal Distance from Beam 2 is: 17 feet.

    Minimum Bridle Point Height will be 80 feet; Maximum Bridle Point Length is 90 feet.

    Baskets will be made from 15 foot split.

    Basic Bridle Length will be 15 feet.

4. The height of Beam 1 is 16.3 inches, the width is 15 inches.

    The height of Beam 2 is 16.3 inches, the width is 15 inches.

    Height above deck is: 88 feet.

    Horizontal Distance from Beam 1 is: 13 feet, Horizontal Distance from Beam 2 is: 19.5 feet.

    Minimum Bridle Point Height will be 55 feet; Maximum Bridle Point Length is 70 feet.

    Baskets will be made from 10 foot steel.

    Basic Bridle Length will be 20 feet.

5. The height of Beam 1 is 22 inches, the width is 24 inches.

    The height of Beam 2 is 22 inches, the width is 24 inches.

    Height above deck is: 87 feet for Beam 1 and 96 feet for Beam 2.

    Horizontal Distance from Beam 1 is: 12.6 feet, Horizontal Distance from Beam 2 is: 14.4 feet.

    Minimum Bridle Point Height will be 65 feet; Maximum Bridle Point Length is 75 feet.

    Baskets will be made from 15 foot split.

    Basic Bridle Length will be 10 feet.

6. The height of Beam 1 is 22 inches, the width is 16 inches.

    The height of Beam 2 is 22 inches, the width is 16 inches.

    Height above deck is: 150 feet for Beam 1 and 150 feet for Beam 2.

    Horizontal Distance from Beam 1 is: 17.2 feet, Horizontal Distance from Beam 2 is: 22.8 feet.

    Minimum Bridle Point Height will be 125 feet; Maximum Bridle Point Length is 130 feet.

    Baskets will be made from 15 foot split.

    Basic Bridle Length will be 30 feet.

7. The height of Beam 1 is 45 inches, the width is 40 inches.

    The height of Beam 2 is 45 inches, the width is 40 inches.

    Height above deck is: 115 feet for both Beams.

    Horizontal Distance from Beam 1 is: 16.4 feet, Horizontal Distance from Beam 2 is: 24.6 feet.

    Minimum Bridle Point Height will be 80 feet; Maximum Bridle Point Length is 90 feet.

    Baskets will be made from 17.5 foot steel.

    Basic Bridle Length will be 25 feet.

8. The height of Beam 1 is 38 inches, the width is 37 inches.

    The height of Beam 2 is 33 inches, the width is 25 inches.

    Height above deck is: 93.5 feet for Beam 1 and 110 feet for Beam 2.

    Horizontal Distance from Beam 1 is: 18.8 feet, Horizontal Distance from Beam 2 is: 19.2 feet.

    Minimum Bridle Point Height will be 60 feet; Maximum Bridle Point Length is 80 feet.

    Baskets will be made from 15 foot split.

    Basic Bridle Length will be 20 feet.

9. The height of Beam 1 is 18 inches, the width is 18.6 inches.

    The height of Beam 2 is 35 inches, the width is 28 inches.

    Height above deck is: 100 feet for Beam 1 and 109 feet for Beam 2.

    Horizontal Distance from Beam 1 is: 3 feet, Horizontal Distance from Beam 2 is: 22 feet.

    Minimum Bridle Point Height will be 65 feet; Maximum Bridle Point Length is 95 feet.

    Baskets will be made from 12.5 foot split.

    Basic Bridle Length will be 25 feet.

10. The height of Beam 1 is 24 inches, the width is 20 inches.

    The height of Beam 2 is 18 inches, the width is 15 inches.

    Height above deck is: 135 feet for Beam 1 and 155 feet for Beam 2.

    Horizontal Distance from Beam 1 is: 23.5 feet, Horizontal Distance from Beam 2 is: 24.5 feet.

    Minimum Bridle Point Height will be 80 feet; Maximum Bridle Point Length is 119 feet.

    Baskets will be made from 15 foot split.

    Basic Bridle Length will be 30 feet.

Answers

1. Leg 1 Total Length= 29.58 ft. Leg 1 will use 1- 20 ft steel and 1- 5 ft steel. Remaining length= 0.0 ft. Number of shackles = 2.

    Leg 2 Total Length = 31.62 ft. Leg 2 will use 1- 20 ft steel and 1- 5 ft steel. Remaining length = 0.0738 ft. Number of shackles = 3. STAC links = 7

    Bridle Angle = 48.1 degrees, Bridle Point = 27.83 below beam and 57.17 ft. above floor.

2. Leg 1 Total Length = 31.51 ft. Leg 1 will use 1- 20 ft steel and 1- 5 ft steel. Remaining length = 0.0 ft. Number of shackles = 2.

    Leg 2 Total Length = 34.17 ft. Leg 2 will use 1- 20 ft steel and 1- 5 ft steel. Remaining length= 0.0986 ft. Number of shackles = 3. STAC links = 9

    Bridle Angle = 44.5 degrees, Bridle Point = 30.20 below beam and 69.80 ft. above floor.

3.   Leg 1 Total Length = 20.50 ft. Leg 1 will use 1- 10 ft steel and 1- 5 ft steel. Remaining length = 0.0 ft. Number of shackles = 2.

     Leg 2 Total Length = 26.16 ft. Leg 2 will use 1- 20 ft steel. Remaining length = 0.0263 ft. Number of shackles= 2. STAC links = 3

     Bridle Angle = 54.7 degrees, Bridle Point = 19.88 below beam and 82.12 ft. above floor.

4.   Leg 1 Total Length = 23.88 ft. Leg 1 will use 1- 20 ft steel. Remaining length = 0.0 ft. Number of shackles = 1.

     Leg 2 Total Length = 27.96 ft. Leg 2 will use 1- 20 ft steel, a 1- 2.5 ft steel. Remaining length = 0.0472 ft. Number of shackles = 3. STAC links = 5

     Bridle Angle = 77.2 degrees, Bridle Point = 20.03 below beam and 67.97 ft. above floor.

5.   Leg 1 Total Length= 15.92 ft. Leg 1 will use 1- 10 ft steel. Remaining length = 0.0 ft. Number of shackles = 1.

     Leg 2 Total Length = 23.63 ft. Leg 2 will use 1- 10 ft steel and 1- 5 ft steel. Remaining length = 0.0924 ft. Number of shackles = 3. STAC links = 9

     Bridle Angle = 71.5 degrees, Bridle Point = 18.73 below beam and 68.27 ft. above floor.

6.   Leg 1 Total Length = 36.31 ft. Leg 1 will use 1- 30 ft steel. Remaining length = 0.0 ft. Number of shackles = 1.

     Leg 2 Total Length = 39.27 ft. Leg 2 will use 1- 30 ft steel and 1- 2.5 steel. Remaining length= 0.0027 ft. Number of shackles = 3. STAC links = 0

     Bridle Angle = 63.8 degrees, Bridle Point = 31.98 below beam and 118.02 ft. above floor.

7.   Leg 1 Total Length= 30.30 ft. Leg 1 will use 1- 20 ft steel and 1- 5 ft steel. Remaining length = 0.0 ft. Number of shackles = 2.

     Leg 2 Total Length = 35.42 ft. Leg 2 will use 1- 30 ft steel. Remaining length = 0.0046 ft. Number of shackles = 2. STAC links = 0

     Bridle Angle = 76.8 degrees, Bridle Point = 25.48 ft below beam and 89.52 ft. above floor.

8.   Leg 1 Total Length= 24.32 ft. Leg 1 will use 1- 20 ft steel. Remaining length = 0.0 ft. Number of shackles = 1.

     Leg 2 Total Length = 37.25 ft. Leg 2 will use 1- 30 ft steel. Remaining length = 0.0700 ft. Number of shackles= 2. STAC links = 7

     Bridle Angle = 61.5 degrees, Bridle Point = 31.92 ft below beam and 61.58 ft. above floor.

9. Leg 1 Total Length = 30.30 ft. Leg 1 will use 1- 20 ft steel and 1- 5 ft steel. Remaining length= 0.0 ft. Number of shackles = 2.

    Leg 2 Total Length = 44.65 ft. Leg 2 will use 1- 30 ft steel and 1- 10 ft steel. Remaining length= 0.0240 ft. Number of shackles= 3. STAC links = 2

    Bridle Angle = 33.9 degrees, Bridle Point = 38.85 ft below beam and 61.15 ft. above floor.

10. Leg 1 Total Length = 36.02 ft. Leg 1 will use 1- 30 ft steel. Remaining length = 0.0 ft. Number of shackles = 1.

    Leg 2 Total Length = 53.27 ft. Leg 2 will use 2- 20 ft steel and 1- 5 ft steel. Remaining length= 0.0450 ft. Number of shackles= 4. STAC links = 4

    Bridle Angle = 53.8 degrees, Bridle Point = 47.30 ft below beam and 87.70 ft. above floor.

The Truss Load Distribution Worksheets

The following problems will ask you to calculate the static and dynamic loads on the rigging points using the Truss Calculator. *Please note that if your answers vary a few pounds different from the answers posted at the end of the worksheet this maybe caused by the placement of your cable runs. Please be sure and check your cable runs carefully.*

1. Two rigging points

A 20.5 x 20.5 x 20' box truss weighs 10 pounds per linear foot. Hoists are two 1 Ton Lodestar Model Ls. Hoist weight is 114 pounds each. Each hoist has 80 feet of chain weighing 1 pound per foot. Hoists will be attached to the truss at the ends. There will be 3- 75 pound movers located 2 feet, 8 feet and 10 feet on the truss. Calculate the static and dynamic load on Point 1 and Point 2. Calculate the Total Static and Dynamic Loads.

2 . Three rigging points

A 12'x 12' x 32 box truss weighs 6 pounds per linear foot. Hoists are two 1/2 Ton Lodestar Model Fs. Hoist weight is 74 pounds each. Each hoist has 80 feet of chain weighing .5 pounds per foot. Hoists will be attached to the truss at the ends and one in the center. The truss is being used as a cable bridge. Cable weighs 8 pounds per foot and will drop 40 feet to the floor off the right side of the truss. Calculate the static and dynamic load on Points 1, 2 and 3. Next, calculate the Total Static and Dynamic Loads.

3. Four rigging points

A 20.5 x 20.5 x 44 ft box truss weighs 10 pounds per linear foot. There is a 4 foot cantilever at both ends of the truss. The hoists are spaced at the 4 foot, 16 foot, 28 foot, and 40 foot intervals. Hoists are 4- 1 Ton Lodestar Model Ls. Hoist speed is 16 feet pet minute. Hoist weight is 114 pounds each. Each hoist has 80 feet of chain weighing 1 pounds per foot.

Lighting Equipment is as follows:

3 - Source 4 Zooms, weight = 21 pounds each. Location: Equally distributed along each of the left cantilever.

3- Source 4 Zooms, weight = 21 pounds each. Location: Equally distributed along each of the right cantilever.

4 - Movers, weight = 75 pounds each equally distributed between Points 1 and 2.

4 - Movers, weight = 75 pounds each equally distributed between Points 2 and 3.

4 - Movers, weight = 75 pounds each equally distributed between Points 3 and 4.

Cable as follows:

There are 3 cable runs along the truss. Cable weight is 3 pounds per linear foot.

Cable 1 starts at the left end of the truss and runs 40 feet.

Cable 2 starts at the left end of the truss and runs 22 feet.

Cable 3 starts at the left end of the truss and runs 4 feet.

Cable Drop is 40 feet.

Calculate the static and dynamic load on Points 1, 2, 3 and 4. Next, calculate the Total Static and Dynamic Loads.

4. Five rigging points

A 20.5 x 20.5 x 45 ft box truss weighs 10 pounds per linear foot. There is a 5 foot cantilever at the Left end of the truss. The hoists are spaced at the 5 foot, 15 foot, 25 foot, 35 foot, and 45 foot intervals. Hoists are 5 - 1 Ton Lodestar Model Ls. Hoist speed is 16 feet pet minute. Hoist weight is 114 pounds each. Each hoist has 80 feet of chain weighing 1 pounds per foot.

Lighting Equipment is as follows:

2 - Movers, weight = 95 pounds each, equally distributed on the Left cantilever.

2 - 6 lamp PAR Bars w/ steel cans. Weight = 70 pounds each. Each PAR Bar 1 is located between Points 1 and 2. PAR Bar 2 is located between Points 2 and 3.

1 - Followspot seat w/ operator weighs 450 pounds and is located equally between Points 3 and 4.

3 - Movers, weight = 80 pounds each, equally distributed between Points 4 and 5.

1 - 50' wire rope ladder, weight = 50 pounds located at Point 5.

Cable as follows:

There are 3 cable runs along the truss. Cable weight is 3 pounds per linear foot and drops 40 off the right end of the truss.

Cable 1 starts at the right end of the truss and runs 45 feet onto the truss.

Cable 2 starts at the right end of the truss and runs 25 feet onto the truss.

Cable 3 starts at the right end of the truss and runs 10 feet onto the truss.

Cable Drop is 40 feet. Calculate the static and dynamic load on Points 1, 2, 3, 4 and 5. Next, calculate the Total Static and Dynamic Loads.

5. Six rigging points

A 20.5 x 30" x 50' box truss weighs 12 pounds per linear foot. The hoists are spaced at the 0 foot, 10 foot, 20 foot, 30 foot, 40 foot and 50 foot intervals. There are no cantilevers. Hoists are 6 - 1 Ton Lodestar Model RRs. Hoist speed is 32 feet per minute. Hoist weight is 114 pounds each. Each hoist has 60 feet of chain weighing 1 pounds per foot. Truss serves as a bridge and connects to a Mother Grid. (See Problem 6). Connected to the truss is a UDL scenic unit that weighs 4,500 pounds and runs the entire length of the truss. Calculate the static and dynamic load on Points 1, 2, 3, 4, 5 and 6. Next, calculate the Total Static and Dynamic Loads.

6. Six rigging points

A 20.5 x 30" x 50' box truss weighs 12 pounds per linear foot. It serves as a Mother Grid for a similar truss (see Problem 5) that will suspend a dynamic load of 32 fpm. The hoists are spaced at the 0 foot, 10 foot, 20 foot, 30 foot, 40 foot and 50 foot intervals. There are no cantilevers. Hoists are 6 - 2 Ton Lodestar Model RRs. Hoist speed is 16 feet per minute. Hoist weight is 112 pounds each. Each hoist has 80 feet of chain weighing 1 pounds per foot. Calculate the static and dynamic load on Points 1, 2, 3, 4, 5 and 6. Next, calculate the Total Static and Dynamic Loads.

7. Seven Rigging Points

A Generic Box Truss is 48 feet long and weighs weighs 10 pounds per linear foot. The hoists are spaced at the 0 foot, 8 foot, 16 foot, 24 foot, 32 foot, 40 foot, and 48 foot intervals. Hoists are 7 - 1 Ton Lodestar Model LS. Hoist speed is 16 feet pet minute. Hoist weight is 114 pounds each. Each hoist has 80 feet of chain weighing 1 pounds per foot.

Lighting Equipment is as follows:

2- follow spot chairs, weight = 450 pounds each with operator. Located midway between Points 3 and 4 and Points 5 and 6

2- PAR Bars, weight = 75 each. Located as a UDL between Points 1 and 2, and 2 and 3.

16 Movers, weight = 90 pounds each and are distributed as follows: 4 - Movers will be a UDL between Points 3 and 4, 4 - Movers will be a UDL between Points 4 and 5, 4 - Movers will be a UDL between Points 5 and 6, and 4 - Movers will be a UDL between Points 6 and 7.

1- 50' wire rope ladder, weight = 50 pounds located at Point 7.

Cable as follows:

There are 4 cable runs along the truss. Cable weight is 3 pounds per linear foot and drops 40 off the right end of the truss.

Cable 1 starts at the right end of the truss and runs 44 feet onto the truss.

Cable 2 starts at the right end of the truss and runs 28 feet onto the truss.

Cable 3 starts at the right end of the truss and runs 20 feet onto the truss.

Cable 4 starts at the right end of the truss and runs 8 feet onto the truss.

Cable Drop is 40 feet. Calculate the static and dynamic load on Points 1, 2, 3, 4, 5, 6, and 7. Next, calculate the Total Static and Dynamic Loads.

8. Two rigging points

A 20.5 x 20.5 x 25' box truss weighs 10 pounds per linear foot. There is a 5-foot cantilever at the right end of the truss. Hoists are two 1 Ton Lodestar Model Ls. Hoist weight is 114 pounds each. Each hoist has 60 feet of chain weighing 1 pound per foot. Hoists will attach to the left end of the truss and 5 feet in from the right end. There will be 4 - 75 pound movers; one is located 16.5 feet, another at 18.5 feet, another at 21.5 feet and the last one at 24 feet on the truss. A 300 pound curtain will hang 10 feet onto the truss from the left side. A single 3 pound per linear foot cable will run 5 feet onto the truss from the right and drop 40 feet to the deck. Calculate the static and dynamic load on Point 1 and Point 2. Calculate the Total Static and Dynamic Loads.

9. Three Rigging Points

A 12'x 12' x 30' box truss weighs 6 pounds per linear foot. The truss cantilevers 5 feet left and 5 feet right making the span 20 feet. Hoists are two 1/2 Ton Lodestar Model Fs. Hoist weight is 74 pounds each. Each hoist has 60 feet of chain weighing .5 pounds per foot. Hoists will be attached to the truss 5 feet in from the ends and one in the center. There is a 400-pound velour curtain that starts at the left end of the truss and runs 10 feet to the right. A 75-pound PAR Bar is centered between Points 2 and 3. Two 16-pound Source 4s are attached to the right cantilever at 26 feet and 28 feet. A multi-cable runs 5 feet onto the right side of the truss and drops 40 feet to the deck. Cable weighs 3 pounds per linear foot. Calculate the static and dynamic load on Points 1, 2 and 3. Next, calculate the Total Static and Dynamic Loads.

10. Four rigging points

A 20.5" x 20.5" x 60' box truss weighs 10 pounds per linear foot. The hoists are spaced at the 0 foot, 20 foot, 40 foot, and 60 foot intervals. Hoists are 4 - 1 Ton Lodestar Model Ls. Hoist speed is 16 feet pet minute. Hoist weight is 114 pounds each. Each hoist has 60 feet of chain weighing 1 pounds per foot.
Lighting Equipment is as follows:
8 - Source 4 Zooms, weight = 22 pounds each. Location: Equally distributed between Points 2 and 3.
3 - Movers, weight = 75 pounds each. Location: 1.5 feet, 3 feet, and 4.5 feet from the left end of the truss.
3 - Movers, weight = 75 pounds each. Location: 41.5 feet, 43 feet, 44.5 feet from the left end of the truss.
1 - Mover, weight = 75 pounds. Location: 55 feet from the left end of the truss.
Cable as follows:
There are 3 cable runs along the truss. Cable weight is 3 pounds per linear foot.
Cable 1 starts at the right end of the truss and runs 50 feet.
Cable 2 starts at the right end of the truss and runs 30 feet.
Cable 3 starts at the right end of the truss and runs 10 feet.
Cable Drop is 35 feet.

Calculate the static and dynamic load on Points 1, 2, 3 and 4. Next, calculate the Total Static and Dynamic Loads.

Answers

1. Point 1 = 444 pounds static load/ 562 pounds dynamic load.
    Point 2 = 369 pounds static load/ 467 pounds dynamic load.
    Total Static Load = 813 pounds. Total Dynamic Load = 1,030 pounds.

2. Point 1 = 226 pounds static load/ 286 pounds dynamic load.
    Point 2 = 338 pounds static load/ 428 pounds dynamic load.
    Point 3 = 546 pounds static load/ 692 pounds dynamic load.
    Total Static Load = 1,110 pounds. Total Dynamic Load = 1,406 pounds.

3. Point 1 = 955 pounds static load/ 1210 pounds dynamic load.
    Point 2 = 550 pounds static load/ 697 pounds dynamic load.
    Point 3 = 638 pounds static load/ 808 pounds dynamic load.
    Point 4 = 542 pounds static load/ 687 pounds dynamic load.
    Total Static Load = 2,686 pounds. Total Dynamic Load = 3,402 pounds.

4. Point 1 = 628 pounds static load/ 795 pounds dynamic load.
    Point 2 = 364 pounds static load/ 461 pounds dynamic load.
    Point 3 = 610 pounds static load/ 702 pounds dynamic load.
    Point 4 = 832 pounds static load/1,053 pounds dynamic load.
    Point 5 = 832 pounds static load/ 1,053 pounds dynamic load.
    Total Static Load = 3,135 pounds. Total Dynamic Load = 3,971 pounds.

5. Point 1 = 684 pounds static load/ 1,049 pounds dynamic load.
    Point 2 = 1,194 pounds static load/ 1,831 pounds dynamic load.
    Point 3 = 1,194 pounds static load/ 1,831 pounds dynamic load.
    Point 4 = 1,194 pounds static load/ 1,831 pounds dynamic load.
    Point 5 = 1,194 pounds static load/ 1,831 pounds dynamic load.
    Point 6 = 684 pounds static load/ 1,049 pounds dynamic load.
    Total Static Load = 6,144 pounds. Total Dynamic Load = 9,421 pounds.

6.   Point 1 = 1,301 pounds static load/ 1,995 pounds dynamic load.
      Point 2 = 2,143 pounds static load/ 3,286 pounds dynamic load.
      Point 3 = 2,143 pounds static load/ 3,286 pounds dynamic load.
      Point 4 = 2,143 pounds static load/ 3,286 pounds dynamic load.
      Point 5 = 2,143 pounds static load/ 3,286 pounds dynamic load.
      Point 6 = 1,301 pounds static load/ 1,995 pounds dynamic load.
      Total Static Load = 11,174 pounds. Total Dynamic Load = 17,133 pounds.

7.   Point 1 = 275 pounds static load/ 348 pounds dynamic load.
      Point 2 = 373 pounds static load/ 472 pounds dynamic load.
      Point 3 = 750 pounds static load/ 949 pounds dynamic load.
      Point 4 = 898 pounds static load/ 1,137 pounds dynamic load.
      Point 5 = 928 pounds static load/ 1,175 pounds dynamic load.
      Point 6 = 943 pounds static load/ 1,175 pounds dynamic load.
      Point 7 = 992 pounds static load/ 1,257 pounds dynamic load.
      Total Static Load = 5,158 pounds. Total Dynamic Load = 6,514 pounds.

8.   Point 1 = 453 pounds static load/ 573 pounds dynamic load.
      Point 2 = 880 pounds static load/ 1,115 pounds dynamic load.
      Total Static Load = 1,333 pounds. Total Dynamic Load = 1,688 pounds.

9.   Point 1 = 572 pounds static load/ 724 pounds dynamic load.
      Point 2 = 115 pounds static load/ 145 pounds dynamic load.
      Point 3 = 448 pounds static load/ 567 pounds dynamic load.
      Total Static Load = 1,134 pounds. Total Dynamic Load= 1,436 pounds.

10.   Point 1 = 473 pounds static load/ 599 pounds dynamic load.
      Point 2 = 556 pounds static load/ 704 pounds dynamic load.
      Point 3 = 792 pounds static load/ 1,003 pounds dynamic load.
      Point 4 = 762 pounds static load 965 pounds dynamic load.
      Total Static Load = 2,582 pounds. Total Dynamic Load = 3,271 pounds.

Bridle Calculator Pro

The following problems will ask you to make up the steel for Legs 1 and Legs 2 using the Bridle Calculator- Pro. The inside length of deck chain will be either 3" or 4" inches. You may set this up in the Setup Menu. The size of the steel will be either 3/8" or 1/2". Shackle size will be determined by the size of the steel selected. These questions are the same questions asked in the Bridle Calculator portion of this Chapter. Compare the answers calculated in the Bridle Calculator- Pro with the answers from the Bridle Calculator. Remember, you will need to enable the macros when you load the Bridle Calculator- Pro and enable the add Inch Calc. Good Luck.

Problems

1. The height of Beam 1 is 12 inches, the width is 9 inches.
   The height of Beam 2 is 12 inches, the width is 9 inches.
   Height above deck is: 80 feet.
   Steel will be 3/8". Shackle size is 5/8". Inside length of STAC chain is 3".
   Horizontal Distance from Beam 1 is: 10 feet, Horizontal Distance from Beam 2 is: 15 feet.
   Minimum Bridle Point Height will be 40 feet; Maximum Bridle Point Length is 67 feet.
   Baskets will be made from 10 foot steel.
   Basic Bridle Length will be 25 feet.

2. The height of Beam 1 is 18 inches, the width is 20 inches.
   The height of Beam 2 is 18 inches, the width is 20 inches.
   Height above deck is: 100 feet.
   Steel will be 3/8". Shackle size is 5/8". Inside length of STAC chain is 3".
   Horizontal Distance from Beam 1 is: 9 feet, Horizontal Distance from Beam 2 is: 16 feet.
   Minimum Bridle Point Height will be 65 feet; Maximum Bridle Point Length is 80 feet.
   Baskets will be made from 15 foot split.
   Basic Bridle Length will be 25 feet.

3. The height of Beam 1 is 32 inches, the width is 26 inches.
   The height of Beam 2 is 32 inches, the width is 26 inches.
   Height above deck is: 102 feet.
   Steel will be 1/2". Shackle size is 3/4". Inside length of STAC chain is 4".
   Horizontal Distance from Beam 1 is: 5 feet, Horizontal Distance from Beam 2 is: 17 feet.
   Bridle Point MUST be at least 80'0" above the deck.
   Baskets will be made from 15 foot split.
   Basic Bridle Length will be 15 feet.

4. The height of Beam 1 is 16.3 inches, the width is 15 inches.

    The height of Beam 2 is 16.3 inches, the width is 15 inches.

    Height above deck is: 88 feet.

    Steel will be 3/8". Shackle size is 5/8". Inside length of STAC chain is 3".

    Horizontal Distance from Beam 1 is: 13 feet, Horizontal Distance from Beam 2 is: 19.5 feet.

    Minimum Bridle Point Height will be 55 feet; Maximum Bridle Point Length is 70 feet.

    Baskets will be made from 10 foot steel.

    Basic Bridle Length will be 20 feet.

5. The height of Beam 1 is 22 inches, the width is 24 inches.

    The height of Beam 2 is 22 inches, the width is 24 inches.

    Height above deck is: 87 feet for Beam 1 and 96 feet for Beam 2.

    Steel will be 3/8". Shackle size is 5/8". Inside length of STAC chain is 3".

    Horizontal Distance from Beam 1 is: 12.6 feet, Horizontal Distance from Beam 2 is: 14.4 feet.

    Minimum Bridle Point Height will be 65 feet; Maximum Bridle Point Length is 75 feet.

    Baskets will be made from 15 foot split.

    Basic Bridle Length will be 10 feet.

6. The height of Beam 1 is 22 inches, the width is 16 inches.

    The height of Beam 2 is 22 inches, the width is 16 inches.

    Height above deck is: 150 feet for Beam 1 and 150 feet for Beam 2.

    Steel will be 3/8". Shackle size is 5/8". Inside length of STAC chain is 3".

    Horizontal Distance from Beam 1 is: 17.2 feet, Horizontal Distance from Beam 2 is: 22.8 feet.

    Minimum Bridle Point Height will be 125 feet; Maximum Bridle Point Length is 130 feet.

    Baskets will be made from 15 foot split.

    Basic Bridle Length will be 30 feet.

7. The height of Beam 1 is 45 inches, the width is 40 inches.

    The height of Beam 2 is 45 inches, the width is 40 inches.

    Height above deck is: 115 feet for both Beams.

    Steel will be 3/8". Shackle size is 5/8". Inside length of STAC chain is 3".

    Horizontal Distance from Beam 1 is: 16.4 feet, Horizontal Distance from Beam 2 is: 24.6 feet.

    Minimum Bridle Point Height will be 80 feet; Maximum Bridle Point Length is 90 feet.

    Baskets will be made from 17.5 foot steel.

    Basic Bridle Length will be 25 feet.

8. The height of Beam 1 is 38 inches, the width is 37 inches.

   The height of Beam 2 is 33 inches, the width is 25 inches.

   Height above deck is: 93.5 feet for Beam 1 and 110 feet for Beam 2.

   Steel will be 1/2". Shackle size is 3/4". Inside length of STAC chain is 4".

   Horizontal Distance from Beam 1 is: 18.8 feet, Horizontal Distance from Beam 2 is: 19.2 feet.

   Minimum Bridle Point Height will be 60 feet; Maximum Bridle Point Length is 80 feet.

   Baskets will be made from 15 foot split.

   Basic Bridle Length will be 20 feet.

9. The height of Beam 1 is 18 inches, the width is 18.6 inches.

   The height of Beam 2 is 35 inches, the width is 28 inches.

   Height above deck is: 100 feet for Beam 1 and 109 feet for Beam 2.

   Horizontal Distance from Beam 1 is: 3 feet, Horizontal Distance from Beam 2 is: 22 feet.

   Steel will be 1/2". Shackle size is 3/4". Inside length of STAC chain is 4".

   Minimum Bridle Point Height will be 65 feet; Maximum Bridle Point Length is 95 feet.

   Baskets will be made from 12.5 foot split.

   Basic Bridle Length will be 25 feet.

10. The height of Beam 1 is 24 inches, the width is 20 inches.

    The height of Beam 2 is 18 inches, the width is 15 inches.

    Height above deck is: 135 feet for Beam 1 and 155 feet for Beam 2.

    Horizontal Distance from Beam 1 is: 23.5 feet, Horizontal Distance from Beam 2 is: 24.5 feet.

    Steel will be 1/2". Shackle size is 3/4". Inside length of STAC chain is 4".

    Minimum Bridle Point Height will be 80 feet; Maximum Bridle Point Length is 119 feet.

    Baskets will be made from 15 foot split.

    Basic Bridle Length will be 30 feet.

Answers

1. Leg 1 will use 1- 20 ft steel and 1- 5 ft steel.

   Leg 2 will use 1- 20 ft steel and 1- 5 ft steel and a 1- 2' steel. STAC links = 0

   Bridle Angle = 49 degrees, Bridle Point = 27'-3" below beam and 52'-9" above floor.

2. Leg 1 will use 1- 20 ft steel and 1- 5 ft steel.

   Leg 2 will use 1- 20 ft steel, 1- 5 ft steel and 1- 2.5' steel. STAC links = 0

   Bridle Angle = 44 degrees, Bridle Point = 30'-3" below the beam and 69'-9" above floor.

3. Leg 1 will use 1- 10 ft steel and 1- 5 ft steel.

    Leg 2 will use 1- 20 ft steel. STAC links = 2

    Bridle Angle = 54 degrees, Bridle Point = 20'-2" below beam and 81'-10" ft. above floor.

4. Leg 1 will use 1- 20 ft steel.

    Leg 2 will use 1- 20 ft steel, a 1- 2.5 ft steel. STAC links = 5

    Bridle Angle = 77 degrees, Bridle Point = 20'-0" below beam and 68'-0" ft. above floor.

5. Leg 1 will use 1- 10 ft steel.

    Leg 2 will use 1- 10 ft steel and 1- 5 ft steel. STAC links = 10

    Bridle Angle = 89 degrees, Bridle Point = 9'-11" below Beam 1 and 77'-1" ft. above floor.

6. Leg 1 will use 1- 30 ft steel.

    Leg 2 will use 1- 30 ft steel and 1- 2.5 steel. STAC links = 5

    Bridle Angle = 64 degrees, Bridle Point = 32'-1" below Beam 1 and 117'-11" ft. above floor.

7. Leg 1 will use 1- 20 ft steel and 1- 5 ft steel.

    Leg 2 will use 1- 30 ft steel. STAC links = 0

    Bridle Angle = 77 degrees, Bridle Point = 25'-6" below beam and 89'-6" above floor.

8. Leg 1 will use 1- 20 ft steel.

    Leg 2 will use 1- 30 ft steel. STAC links = 5

    Bridle Angle = 81 degrees, Bridle Point = 15'-9" ft below Beam 1 and 77'-9" ft. above floor.

9. Leg 1 will use 1- 20 ft steel and 1- 5 ft steel.

    Leg 2 will use 1- 30 ft steel and 1- 10 ft steel. STAC links = 2

    Bridle Angle = 35 degrees, Bridle Point = 30'-5" below Beam 1 and 69'-7" above floor.

10. Leg 1 will use 1- 30 ft steel.

    Leg 2 will use 1- 30 ft steel, 1- 10' steel and 1- 5' steel. STAC links = 3

    Bridle Angle = 68 degrees, Bridle Point = 27'-7" below Beam 1 and 107'-5" above floor.

Chapter 21:

Calculating Bridle Length with Little or No Math

The Give-and-Take Method of Calculating Bridle Lengths (for beams at the same height)

This method is called Give-and-Take because we will add length to one bridle leg, and take away the same distance from the other leg. What we need to calculate is the length to add and subtract. To do this we have to know the vertical distance that the apex is from the center of the Span (where it is in our reference bridle).

This method requires that you compare the "desired bridle" to a "reference bridle." This reference bridle has legs that are equal length, so the apex is centered between the beams. The length of the legs is proportional to the Span distance, and is either 100% of the Span distance, 70% of the Span distance (Span distance times 0.7), or 60% of the Span distance (Span distance times 0.6). Which length you choose is dependent on the height of the steel and the minimum hook height required. However, the smaller the percentage, the flatter the bridle, and the greater the force on the beams. So, when possible, use the steepest (longest) bridle possible.

The table below shows the approximate bridle angle using the percentages of the Span discussed above. Remember, the bridle angle should NEVER exceed 120 degrees.

Leg Length compared to Span	Approximate Bridle Angle
100%	60 degrees
70%	90 degrees
60%	120 degrees

The formulas to calculate the leg lengths are slightly different depending on which of the three reference bridles you use. The easiest one is the reference bridle whose legs are 100% of the Span.

Long Leg Length = Span + (Off-center Distance /2)

Short Leg Length = Span - (Off-center Distance /2)

So, plugging the numbers from our example into the formulas, we get:

Long Leg Length = 24 + (6/2)

Long Leg Length = 24 + 3

Long Leg Length = 27 feet

Short Leg Length = 24 - (6 /2)

Short Leg Length = 24 - 3

Short Leg Length = 21 feet

Now, to make these bridle legs we need to subtract the ELOH for the basket lengths. So if we are using 5-foot baskets, we get:

Long Leg Length = 5B/19

Short Leg Length = 5B/25

If the apex is too low when using the 100% reference bridle, then you may have to use either the 70% or 60% reference bridles. When you use these reference bridles, the formulas are:

Long Leg Length = (Span x 0.7) + (Off-center Distance x 0.7)

Short Leg Length = (Span x 0.7) - (Off-center Distance x 0.7)

and

Long Leg Length = (Span x 0.6) + (Off-center Distance x 0.6)

Short Leg Length = (Span x 0.6) - (Off-center Distance x 0.6)

respectively. So, using the same example with a 70% Reference Bridle, we get:

Long Leg Length = (24 x 0.7) + (6 x 0.7)

Long Leg Length = 16.8 + 4.2

Long Leg Length = 21 feet

Short Leg Length = (24 x 0.7) - (6 x 0.7)

Short Leg Length = 16.8 - 4.2

Short Leg Length = 12.6 feet

Problems

1. Horizontal Distance from Beam 1 is: 10 feet, Horizontal Distance from Beam 2 is: 15 feet.
   Basket length = 5 feet
   Approximate bridle angle = 60 degrees
   Find the Span, the Offset distance of the Apex, the ELOH, Length of Short Leg, Length of Long Leg, Length of Short Leg- ELOH, Length of Long Leg - ELOH

2. Horizontal Distance from Beam 1 is: 9 feet, Horizontal Distance from Beam 2 is: 16 feet.
   Basket length = 10 feet
   Approximate bridle angle = 90 degrees
   Find the Span, the Offset distance of the Apex, the ELOH, Length of Short Leg, Length of Long Leg, Length of Short Leg- ELOH, Length of Long Leg - ELOH

3. Horizontal Distance from Beam 1 is: 5 feet, Horizontal Distance from Beam 2 is: 9 feet.
   Basket length = 5 feet
   Approximate bridle angle = 120 degrees
   Find the Span, the Offset distance of the Apex, the ELOH, Length of Short Leg, Length of Long Leg, Length of Short Leg- ELOH, Length of Long Leg - ELOH

4. Horizontal Distance from Beam 1 is: 4.1 feet, Horizontal Distance from Beam 2 is: 5.9 feet.
   Basket length = 5 feet
   Approximate bridle angle = 90 degrees
   Find the Span, the Offset distance of the Apex, the ELOH, Length of Short Leg, Length of Long Leg, Length of Short Leg- ELOH, Length of Long Leg – ELOH

5. Horizontal Distance from Beam 1 is: 5.3 feet, Horizontal Distance from Beam 2 is: 5.7 feet.
   Basket length = 10 feet
   Approximate bridle angle = 60 degrees
   Find the Span, the Offset distance of the Apex, the ELOH, Length of Short Leg, Length of Long Leg, Length of Short Leg- ELOH, Length of Long Leg – ELOH

6. Horizontal Distance from Beam 1 is: 7.3 feet, Horizontal Distance from Beam 2 is: 8.4 feet.
   Basket length = 10 feet
   Approximate bridle angle = 90 degrees
   Find the Span, the Offset distance of the Apex, the ELOH, Length of Short Leg, Length of Long Leg, Length of Short Leg- ELOH, Length of Long Leg – ELOH

7. Horizontal Distance from Beam 1 is: 11.3 feet, Horizontal Distance from Beam 2 is: 13.5 feet.
    Basket length = 15 feet
    Approximate bridle angle = 60 degrees
    Find the Span, the Offset distance of the Apex, the ELOH, Length of Short Leg, Length of Long
    Leg, Length of Short Leg- ELOH, Length of Long Leg – ELOH

8. Horizontal Distance from Beam 1 is: 12.8 feet, Horizontal Distance from Beam 2 is: 14.3 feet.
    Basket length = 15 feet
    Approximate bridle angle = 90 degrees
    Find the Span, the Offset distance of the Apex, the ELOH, Length of Short Leg, Length of Long
    Leg, Length of Short Leg- ELOH, Length of Long Leg – ELOH

9. Horizontal Distance from Beam 1 is: 3.3 feet, Horizontal Distance from Beam 2 is: 4.2 feet.
    Basket length = 5 feet
    Approximate bridle angle = 120 degrees
    Find the Span, the Offset distance of the Apex, the ELOH, Length of Short Leg, Length of Long
    Leg, Length of Short Leg- ELOH, Length of Long Leg – ELOH

10. Horizontal Distance from Beam 1 is: 8.8 feet, Horizontal Distance from Beam 2 is: 10.4 feet.
    Basket length = 10 feet
    Approximate bridle angle = 90 degrees
    Find the Span, the Offset distance of the Apex, the ELOH, Length of Short Leg, Length of Long
    Leg, Length of Short Leg- ELOH, Length of Long Leg – ELOH

Answers

1. Span= 25 ft
    Offset distance of Apex = 2.5 ft
    Short Leg = 23.75 ft
    Long Leg = 26.25 ft
    Short Leg Length-ELOH = 21.75 ft
    Long Leg Length-ELOH = 24.25 ft

2. Span = 25 ft
    Off set distance of Apex = 3.5 ft
    Short Leg = 15.05 ft
    Long Leg = 19.95 ft
    Short Leg Length-ELOH = 12.05 ft
    Long Leg Length-ELOH = 16.95 ft

3. Span = 14 ft
    Off set distance of Apex = 2 ft
    Short Leg = 7.2 ft
    Long Leg = 9.6 ft
    Short Leg Length-ELOH = 5.2 ft
    Long Leg Length-ELOH = 7.6 ft

4. Span = 10 ft
    Off set distance of Apex = .9 ft
    Short Leg = 6.37 ft
    Long Leg = 7.63 ft
    Short Leg Length-ELOH = 4.37 ft
    Long Leg Length-ELOH = 5.63 ft

5. Span = 11 ft
    Off set distance of Apex = .2 ft
    Short Leg = 10.9 ft
    Long Leg = 11.1 ft
    Short Leg Length-ELOH = 7.9 ft
    Long Leg Length-ELOH = 8.1 ft

6. Span = 15.7 ft
    Off set distance of Ape x = .55 ft
    Short Leg = 10.605 ft
    Long Leg = 11.375 ft
    Short Leg Length-ELOH = 7.605 ft
    Long Leg Length-ELOH = 8.375 ft

7. Span = 24.8 ft
    Off set distance of Apex = 1.1 ft
    Short Leg = 24.25 ft
    Long Leg = 25.35 ft
    Short Leg Length-ELOH = 19.25 ft
    Long Leg Length-ELOH = 20.35 ft

8. Span = 27.1 ft
    Off set distance of Apex = .75 ft
    Short Leg = 18.445 ft
    Long Leg = 19.495 ft
    Short Leg Length-ELOH = 13.445 ft
    Long Leg Length-ELOH = 14.495 ft

9. Span = 7.5 ft
    Off set distance of Apex = .45 ft
    Short Leg = 4.23 ft
    Long Leg = 4.77 ft
    Short Leg Length-ELOH = 2.23 ft
    Long Leg Length-ELOH = 2.77 ft

10. Span = 19.2 ft
    Off set distance of Apex = .8 ft
    Short Leg = 12.88 ft
    Long Leg = 14 ft
    Short Leg Length-ELOH = 9.88 ft
    Long Leg Length-ELOH = 11 ft

One Leg Adjustment Method (for Beams at the Same Height)

This method can be used two ways:
1) Add length to one leg, or 2) Subtract length from one leg

This method is based on adding or removing a percentage of the Span to/from one leg. To understand both how this works, and the distortion that occurs, look at the tables below. In this example, will will be using a Span of 20 feet, so we start with a reference bridle that has two 20-foot long legs and show changes of one leg in 12" increments (5% changes).

Adding length to one leg

Leg length	Add Length	% of Span	Off-center Distance
20'	0"	100%	0"
21'	12"	105%	12"
22'	12"	110%	12.6"
23'	12"	115%	13.2"
24'	12"	120%	13.8"
25'	12"	125%	14.4"
Total	**60"**		**66"**

Subtracting length from one leg

Leg length	Add Length	% of Span	Off-center Distance
20'	0"	100%	0"
19'	12"	95%	12"
18'	12"	90%	11.4"
17'	12"	85%	10.8"
16'	12"	80%	10.2"
15'	12"	75%	9.6"
Total	**60"**		**54"**

Problems

11. If the span between beams is 20 ft, how many links of 4" STAC chain will move the apex 12 inches?

12. If the span between beams is 20 ft, how many links of 4" STAC chain will move the apex 8 inches?

13. If the span between beams is 20 ft, how many links of 4" STAC chain will move the apex 16 inches?

Answers

11. 3 Links

12. 2 Links

13. 4 Links

Beams at Different Heights

The 90% Rule
Short Leg Length = Span
Long Leg Length = Span + (Rise x 0.9)

The 80% Rule
Short Leg Length = Span
Long Leg Length = Span - (Rise x 0.8)

Use the 90% Rule if: Rise is greater than 40% of the Span
Use the 90% Rule if: Rise is 40% of the Span or less

Example: If the low beam is 80 feet above the deck and the high beam is 90 feet above the deck, the Rise is 10 feet. If the Span is 20 feet, then the Rise is 50% of the Span, so use the 90% Rule. so, the lengths of the legs will be:
Short Leg Length = 20 feet

Long Leg Length = 20 + (10 x 0.9)
Long Leg Length = 20 + 9
Long Leg Length = 29 feet

Problems

14. If the low beam is 75 feet above the deck, the high beam is 90 feet above the deck and the Span is 20 feet, calculate the Short Leg and the Long Leg. Choose either the 80% or 90% Rule.

15. If the low beam is 90 feet above the deck, the high beam is 100 feet above the deck and the Span is 30 feet, calculate the Short Leg and the Long Leg. Choose either the 80% or 90% Rule.

16. If the low beam is 60 feet above the deck, the high beam is 67 feet above the deck and the Span is 10 feet, calculate the Short Leg and the Long Leg. Choose either the 80% or 90% Rule.

17. If the low beam is 84 feet above the deck, the high beam is 90 feet above the deck and the Span is 36 feet, calculate the Short Leg and the Long Leg. Choose either the 80% or 90% Rule.

18. If the low beam is 45 feet above the deck, the high beam is 52 feet above the deck and the Span is 15 feet, calculate the Short Leg and the Long Leg. Choose either the 80% or 90% Rule.

19. If the low beam is 80 feet above the deck, the high beam is 93 feet above the deck and the Span is 22 feet, calculate the Short Leg and the Long Leg. Choose either the 80% or 90% Rule.

20. If the low beam is 56 feet above the deck, the high beam is 64.8 feet above the deck and the Span is 18 feet, calculate the Short Leg and the Long Leg. Choose either the 80% or 90% Rule.

Answers

14. Rise = 75%of Span
    Short Leg = 20 feet
    Long Leg = 20 + (15x0.9)
    Long Leg = 33.5 feet

15. Rise = 33.33% of Span
    Short Leg = 30 feet
    Long Leg = 30 + (10x0.8)
    Long Leg = 38 feet

16. Rise= 70% of Span
    Short Leg=10 feet
    Long Leg= 10 + (7x0.9)
    Long Leg = 16.3 feet

17. Rise = 16.666% of Span
    Short Leg =36 feet
    Long Leg = 36 + (6x0.8)
    Long Leg = 40.8 feet

18. Rise = 46.666% of Span
    Short Leg =15 feet
    Long Leg = 15 + (7x0.9)
    Long Leg = 21.3 feet

19. Rise = 59.09% of Span
    Short Leg = 22 feet
    Long Leg = 22 + (13x0.9)
    Long Leg = 33.7 feet

20. Rise = 44.44% of Span
    Short Leg =18 feet
    Long Leg = 18 + (8.8x0.9)
    Long Leg = 25.92 feet

Chapter 22:

How much load can I put on a truss?

This lesson teaches users to calculate the downward force at the center point of the span of a truss. In order to do this calculation, you need to know:

Load = Weight of the Point Load

Location of Point Load = Where on the truss the Load is hung. In this case, it will be a number between 0 (one end of the truss) and 40 (the other end).

Center of Truss = Half of the Span distance. It this example it is 20.

Distance from Location of Point Load to Center of Truss = Well, the Distance from Location of Point Load to Center of Truss

If the Load = 500 pounds and the Location of Point Load = 12 feet. Then,

Load = 500
Location of Point Load = 12
Center of Truss = 20
Distance from Location of Point Load to Center of Truss = 8

To make the calculation easier, we break the calculation into two parts. First, we calculate a "Divisor." The formula for the Divisor is:

Divisor = Center Point / (Center Point - Distance from Location of Point Load to Center of Truss

So,

Divisor = 20/(20-8)

Divisor = 20/12

Divisor = 1.6666667

After we have the Divisor, the second part of the formula is simple.

Downward Force at Center Point = Load/Divisor

So,

Downward Force at Center Point = 500/1.666667

Downward Force at Center Point = 300 pounds

REMEMBER TO ALWAYS CHECK WITH THE TRUSS MANUFACTURER'S LOAD TABLES.

Problems

1. What is the downward force at the center point of a 20- foot long truss with a 350-pound point load at 18 feet?

2. What is the downward force at the center point of a 10- foot long truss with a 500-pound point load at 4 feet?

3. What is the downward force at the center point of a 25- foot long truss with 1,200-pound point load at 20 feet?

4. What is the downward force at the center point of a 20- foot long truss with 540-pound point load at 16 feet, and a 680- pound point load at 5 feet?

5. What is the downward force at the center point of a 15- foot long truss with 600-pound point load at 10 feet, and a 650-point point load at 5 feet?

6. What is the downward force at the center point of a 20- foot long truss with 204-pound point load at 5 feet, a 280-point point load at 8 feet, and a 55- pound point load at 14 feet?

7. What is the downward force at the center point of a 28- foot long truss with 222-pound point load at 9 feet, a 321-point load at 22 feet, and a 298- pound point load at 27 feet?

8. What is the downward force at the center point of a 20- foot long truss with 87-pound point load at 4 feet, an 89- pound point load at 10 feet, a 100- pound point load at 15 feet, and a 98- pound point load at 18 feet?

9. What is the downward force at the center point of a 18- foot long truss with 102-pound point load at 2 feet, an 121- pound point load at 7 feet, a 105- pound point load at 13 feet, and 174- pound point load at 15 feet, and a 200- pound point load at 18 feet?

10. What is the downward force at the center point of a 25- foot long truss with 108-pound point load at 3 feet, an 200- pound point load at 9 feet, a 208- pound point load at 12 feet, a 187- pound point load at 18 feet, and a 300- pound point load at 25 feet?

11. What is the downward force at the center point of a 12- foot long truss with 35-pound point load at 2 feet, a 35- pound point load at 4 feet, a 67- pound point load at 6 feet, a 82- pound point load at 8 feet, a 21- pound point load at 10 feet, a 12- pound point load at 12 feet, a 90- pound point load at 6 feet, and a 100- pound point load at 12 feet?

12. What is the downward force at the center point of a 25- foot long truss with 18-pound point load at 2 feet, a 28- pound point load at 4 feet, a 32- pound point load at 6 feet, a 75- pound point load at 8 feet, a 45- pound point load at 10 feet, a 84- pound point load at 12 feet, a 90- pound point load at 12 feet, and a 22- pound point load at 14 feet, and a 100- pound point load at 23 feet?

13. What is the downward force at the center point of a 24- foot long truss with 80-pound point load at 2 feet, a 40- pound point load at 4 feet, and a 90- pound point load at 6 feet, a 100- pound point load at 18 feet, and a 200- pound point load at 22 feet?

14. What is the downward force at the center point of a 30- foot long truss with 50-pound point load at 8 feet, a 400- pound point load at 12 feet, a 35- pound point load at 16 feet, and a 29- pound point load at 23 feet?

15. What is the downward force at the center point of a 40- foot long truss with 189-pound point load at 14 feet, a 156- pound point load at 23 feet, and a 278- pound point load at 40 feet?

16. What is the downward force at the center point of a 24- foot long truss with 356-pound point load at 2.6 feet, a 221- pound point load at 5.9 feet, and a 432- pound point load at 19.3 feet?

17. What is the downward force at the center point of a 16- foot long truss with 154.6-pound point load at 2.3 feet, a 143.7- pound point load at 7.4 feet, a 176.3- pound point load at 12.8 feet, and a 334.2- pound point load at 15.2 feet?

18. What is the downward force at the center point of a 12- foot long truss with 349.2-pound point load at 2 feet, a 258.4- pound point load at 8.3 feet, and a 437.3- pound point load at 11.4 feet?

19. What is the downward force at the center point of a 50- foot long truss with 265.5-pound point load at 8.3 feet, a 257.8- pound point load at 17.5 feet, a 285.3- pound point load at 32.4 feet, and a 498.2- pound point load at 46.9 feet?

20. What is the downward force at the center point of a 45- foot long truss with 398.4-pound point load at 5.5 feet, a 358.7- pound point load at 14 feet, a 578.2- pound point load at 27.5 feet, and a 238.2- pound point load at 44 feet?

Answers

1. Center point = 70 lb

2. Center point = 400 lb

3. Center point = 480 lb

4. Center point = 556 lb

5. Center point = 833.33 lb

6. Center point = 359 lb

7. Center point = 301.5 lb

8. Center point = 193.4 lb

9. Center point = 233.1 lb

10. Center point = 474.3 lb

11. Center point = 253.6 lb

12. Center point = 232.96 lb

13. Center point = 155 lb

14. Center point = 392.8 lb

15. Center point = 264.9 lb

16. Center point = 354.9 lb

17. Center point = 281.31 lb

18. Center point = 319.47 lb

19. Center point = 531.23 lb

20. Center point = 780.87 lb

Unit VI:
Static and Dynamic Forces

Introduction

In the Introduction to Unit VI, the equation for calculating the force of an accelerating body is discussed. It is:

$$Force = Weight \times \frac{acceleration\ of\ gravity + acceleration\ rate}{acceleration\ of\ gravity}$$

We know that the acceleration of gravity is 32 feet per second^2, but what is the acceleration rate?

Finding the acceleration rate involves applying a specific force for a length of time.

Example: If an object takes 4 seconds to accelerate from a stationary position to moving at 16 feet per second, then: $\frac{16\ feet\ per\ second}{4\ seconds}$ = 4 feet per second, per second, or **4 feet per second^2** is the acceleration rate.

So, if the object weighs 500 pounds, then:

$$Force = Weight \times \frac{acceleration\ of\ gravity + acceleration\ rate}{acceleration\ of\ gravity}$$

$$Force = 500\ lb \times \frac{32\ feet\ per\ second^2 + 4\ feet\ per\ second^2}{32\ feet\ per\ second^2}$$

$$Force = 500\ lb \times \frac{36\ feet\ per\ second^2}{32\ feet\ per\ second^2}$$

$$Force = 500\ lb \times 1.125$$

$Force = 562.5\ lb$

Problems

1. It takes an object 3 seconds to reach a velocity of 8 feet per second. Calculate the instantaneous rate of acceleration.

2. It takes an object 6 seconds to reach a velocity of 20 feet per second. Calculate the instantaneous rate of acceleration.

3. It takes an object 4 seconds to reach a velocity of 16 feet per second. Calculate the instantaneous rate of acceleration.

4. It takes an object 12 seconds to reach a velocity of 23 feet per second. Calculate the instantaneous rate of acceleration.

5. It takes an object 1 second to reach a velocity of 14 feet per second. Calculate the instantaneous rate of acceleration.

6. It takes an object 2.5 seconds to reach a velocity of 13 feet per second. Calculate the instantaneous rate of acceleration.

7. It takes an object 5.6 seconds to reach a velocity of 21 feet per second. Calculate the instantaneous rate of acceleration.

8. An object weighs 350-pounds while at rest on the deck. It accelerates at a velocity of 4 feet per second, per second upward to 16 feet per second. Calculate the dynamic load to an object during its upward acceleration.

9. An object weighs 459-pounds while at rest on the deck. It accelerates at a velocity of 2.34 feet per second, per second upward to 15 feet per second. Calculate the dynamic load to an object during its upward acceleration.

10. What is the rate of acceleration in feet per second, per second of a 16 FPM chain hoist?

11. What is the rate of acceleration in feet per second, per second of a 32 FPM chain hoist?

12. What is the dynamic force caused by moving a 2,050 lb load using a 16 FPM hoist?

13. What is the dynamic force caused by moving a 4,503 lb load using a 16 FPM hoist?

14. What is the dynamic force caused by moving a 2,409 lb load using a 32 FPM hoist?

15. What is the dynamic force caused by moving a 1,943 lb load using a 32 FPM hoist?

16. What is the dynamic force caused by moving a 3,829 lb load using a 16 FPM hoist?

17. Two hoists located at each end of a span are lifting a 1800-pound UDL. The UDL is spaced along a 12- foot span. The acceleration rate of the hoists is 16 FPM. What is the dynamic load on each hoist?

18. Two hoists located at each end of a span are lifting a 3,848-pound UDL. The UDL is spaced along a 10- foot span. The acceleration rate of the hoists is 32 FPM. What is the dynamic load on each hoist?

19. A 378-pound scenic piece is loaded onto a stage elevator. The elevator ascends at a rate of 25 feet-per-second to the stage. It will take 6 seconds to accelerate from a dead stop to a velocity of 25 feet-per-second.
    1. Calculate the instantaneous rate of acceleration.
    2. Calculate the dynamic load during the 4-second upward-acceleration period.

20. A 804.5-pound scenic piece is loaded onto a stage elevator. The elevator ascends at a rate of 13 feet-per-second to the stage. It will take 5.4 seconds to accelerate from a dead stop to a velocity of 13 feet-per-second.
    1. Calculate the instantaneous rate of acceleration.
    2. Calculate the dynamic load during the 4-second upward-acceleration period.

Answers

1. Rate of acceleration = 2.6666 fps^2

2. Rate of acceleration = 3.3333 fps^2

3. Rate of acceleration = 4 fps^2

4. Rate of acceleration = 1.9166 fps^2

5. Rate of acceleration = 14 fps^2

6. Rate of acceleration = 5.2 fps^2

7. Rate of acceleration = 3.75 fps^2

8. Dynamic Load= 393.75 lb

9. Dynamic Load = 492.56 lb

10. 0.266666667 fps^2

11. 0.533333333 fps^2

12. The dynamic force = 2067.08 lb

13. The dynamic force = 4540.52 lb

14. The dynamic force = 2449.15 lb

15. The dynamic force = 1975.38 lb

16. The dynamic force = 3860.90 lb

17. Dynamic load on each hoist is = 907.499 lb

18. Dynamic load on each hoist is = 1956.06 lb

19. 1. Rate of Acceleration = 4.166 fps^2
    2. Dynamic Load= 427.21 lb

20. 1. Rate of Acceleration = 2.407 fps^2
    2. Dynamic Load = 865.01 lb

Chapter 23:

Forces and Design Factor

Equations:

$$Working\ Load\ Limit = \frac{Breaking\ Strength}{Design\ Factor}$$

$$Breaking\ Strength = Working\ Load\ Limit \times Design\ Factor$$

$$Design\ Factor = \frac{Breaking\ Strength}{Load}$$

Note: Design Factors are often expresses as a ratio (example 5:1).

<u>Problems</u>

1. What is the Working Load Limit (WLL) of a piece of hardware with a Breaking Strength (BS) of 1,400 pounds based on a Design Factor of 5:1?

2. What is the Working Load Limit (WLL) of a piece of hardware with a Breaking Strength (BS) of 2,600 pounds based on a Design Factor of 8:1?

3. What is the Working Load Limit (WLL) of a piece of hardware with a Breaking Strength (BS) of 4,500 pounds based on a Design Factor of 10:1?

4. A piece of rigging hardware has a Breaking Strength (BS) of 2000 pounds and is carrying a load of 400 pounds. What is the Design Factor (DF) of the piece of hardware?

5. A piece of rigging hardware has a Breaking Strength (BS) of 10,000 pounds and is carrying a load of 2,300 pounds. What is the Design Factor (DF) of the piece of hardware?

6. A piece of rigging hardware has a Breaking Strength (BS) of 8,500 pounds and is carrying a load of 1,700 pounds. What is the Design Factor (DF) of the piece of hardware?

7. What is the standard Design Factor (DF) given for standing rigging?

8. What is the standard Design Factor (DF) given for running rigging?

9. What is the standard Design Factor (DF) given to rigging when flying people and/or flying or moving objects over the heads of people?

10. Recreational climbing hardware such as carabineers and slings have their Breaking Strength marked in

_____.

Answers

1. 280 lb
2. 325 lb
3. 450 lb
4. 5:1
5. 4.3:1

6. 5:1
7. 5:1
8. 8:1
9. 10:1
10. kiloNewtons

Chapter 24:

Estimating the Stretch of Wire and Fiber Rope under a Static Load

Wire Rope

An estimate of the elastic stretch of wire rope can be calculated by using the following formula:

$$Elastic\ Stretch = \frac{Weight \times "G"\ Factor}{Diameter\ of\ Wire\ Rope^2}$$

"G" Factor = See Chart Below

Cable/Wire Rope	"G" Factor	Cable/Wire Rope	"G" Factor
1x7 302/304 SST	0.00000735	1x7 Galvanized	0.00000661
1x19 302/304 SST	0.00000779	1x19 Galvanized	0.00000698
7x7 302/304 SST	0.0000120	7x7 Galvanized	0.0000107
7x19 302/304 SST	0.0000162	7x19 Galvanized	0.0000140
6x19 302/304 SST IWRC	0.0000157	6x19 Galvanized IWRC	0.0000136
6x25 302/304 SST IWRC	0.0000160	6x25 Galvanized IWRC	0.0000144
19x7 302/304 SST	0.0000197	19x7 Galvanized	0.0000 178

Fiber Rope

The table in Lesson 24 contains elongation information on a few ropes manufactured by New England Ropes at 10, 20, and 30 percent of the rated tensile strength of the rope. For example: placing a 350 pound load on a length of 3/8" diameter Multiline II rope (10 percent of the tensile strength) would cause it to stretch 1.7 percent (0.017) of its length. If you used a 50-foot rope (600 inches) then:

Stretch = 0.017 x 600
Stretch = 10.2 inches

Problems

1. If you hang a 1300-pound load on a 300-foot long piece of 1/2" carbon steel 6x19 Galvanized IWRC, calculate what percentage will stretch? How many inches will it stretch?

2. If you hang a 3000-pound load on a 254-foot long piece of 3/4" carbon steel 19x7 GAC, calculate what percentage it stretch? How many inches will it stretch?

3. If you hang a 434-pound load on a 64-foot long piece of 1/4" stainless steel 7x7 302/304 SST, calculate what percentage it stretch? How many inches will it stretch?

4. If you hang a 759-pound load on a 100-foot long piece of 5/8" steel 1x17 GAC, calculate what percentage it stretch? How many inches will it stretch?

5. If you hang a 1284-pound load on a 75-foot long piece of 1/2" steel 7x7 GAC, calculate what percentage it stretch? How many inches will it stretch?

6. If you hang a 10,000-pound load on a 50-foot long piece of 3/4" stainless steel 6x19 SST IWRC, calculate what percentage it stretch? How many inches will it stretch?

7. If you hang a 1850-pound load on a 35-foot long piece of 3/8" steel 7x19 GAC, calculate what percentage it stretch? How many inches will it stretch?

8. If you hang a 2698.5-pound load on a 80-foot long piece of 1/2" stainless steel 19x7 302/304 SST, calculate what percentage it stretch? How many inches will it stretch?

9. If you hang a 8045-pound load on a 104-foot long piece of 3/4" stainless steel 1x19 302/304 SST,

calculate what percentage it stretch? How many inches will it stretch?

10. If you hang a 154-pound load on a 25-foot long piece of 1/8" steel 6x25 GAC IWRC, calculate what percentage it stretch? How many inches will it stretch?

11. How much stretch (elongation) would occur if you placed a 2000 lb weight on a 60-foot length of 5/8" diameter Sta-Set rope at 20% of its tensile strength?

12. How much stretch (elongation) would occur if you placed a 10,000 lb weight on a 45-foot length of 7/8" diameter Premium 3-Strand Nylon rope at 10% of its tensile strength?

13. How much stretch (elongation) would occur if you placed a 437 lb weight on a 35-foot length of 1/2" diameter 3-Strand Spun Poly rope at 30% of its tensile strength?

14. How much stretch (elongation) would occur if you placed an 870 lb weight on a 26-foot length of 3/8" diameter Multiline II rope at 10% of its tensile strength?

15. How much stretch (elongation) would occur if you placed a 589 lb weight on a 75-foot length of 3/4" diameter Multiline II rope at 20% of its tensile strength?

16. How much stretch (elongation) would occur if you placed a 430 lb weight on a 50-foot length of 9/16" diameter Premium 3-Strand Nylon rope at 30% of its tensile strength?

17. How much stretch (elongation) would occur if you placed a 578 lb weight on a 25-foot length of 7/16" diameter Sta-Set rope at 10% of its tensile strength?

18. How much stretch (elongation) would occur if you placed a 2300 lb weight on a 57-foot length of 1/2" diameter Premium 3-Strand Nylon rope at 20% of its tensile strength?

19. How much stretch (elongation) would occur if you placed a 1650 lb weight on a 100-foot length of 1/2" diameter 3-Strand Spun Poly rope at 10% of its tensile strength?

20. How much stretch (elongation) would occur if you placed an 480 lb weight on a 80-foot length of 3/8" diameter Multiline II rope at 10% of its tensile strength?

Answers

1. Elastic Stretch = 0.07072%
   Stretch in inches = 0.21216

2. Elastic Stretch = 0.09493333%
   Stretch in inches = 0.24113067

3. Elastic Stretch = 0.083328%
   Stretch in inches = 0.05332992

4. Elastic Stretch = 0.01284349%
   Stretch in inches = 0.01284349

5. Elastic Stretch = 0.0549552%
   Stretch in inches = 0.0412164

6. Elastic Stretch = 0.27911111%
   Stretch in inches = 0.13955556

7. Elastic Stretch = 0.18417778%
   Stretch in inches = 0.06446222

8. Elastic Stretch = 0.2126418%
   Stretch in inches = 0.17011344

9. Elastic Stretch = 0.11141431%
   Stretch in inches = 0.11587088

10. Elastic Stretch = 0.1419264%
    Stretch in inches = 0.0354816

11. 20 inches x 2.0 = 1440 inches

12. 540 inches x 5.3 = 2862 inches

13. 420 inches x 7.3 = 3066 inches

14. 312 inches x 1.7 = 530.4 inches

15. 900 inches x 3.7 = 3330 inches

16. 600 inches x 13.1 = 7860 inches

17. 300 inches x .7 = 210 inches

18. 684 inches x 10.4 = 7113.6 inches

19. 1200 inches x 3600 = inches

20. 960 inches x 1.7 = 1632 inches

Chapter 25:

Shock Loads

A shock load is the force that results when an object suddenly accelerates or decelerates, but we most often associate it with the abrupt stop of a falling object. This teaches how to calculated the approximate shock load that results from a falling object being caught by a "line." In this case, the "line" can be a steel wire rope, a fiber rope, or a chain.

Fall Protection

Before we get to specific lines, let calculate the shock load for a general fall. The equation for solving this problem is

$$Force = Weight \times \left(\frac{Free\ Fall\ Distance}{Stopping\ Distance} + 1 \right)$$

Example: A 200-pound man wearing a safety harness and lanyard falls six feet. As he stops, the harness and lanyard stretch 6 inches (or .5 feet). What is the force on him and the rigging that supports him?

Note: Remember to keep all measurements in the same unit of measurement – FEET.

$$Force = Weight \times \left(\frac{Free\ Fall\ Distance}{Stopping\ Distance} + 1 \right)$$

$$Force = Weight \times \left(\frac{6}{0.5} + 1 \right)$$

$$Force = 200 \times (12 + 1)$$

$$Force = 200 \times 13$$

$$\mathbf{Force = 2,600\ lb}$$

Problems

1. A 200-pound man wearing a safety harness and lanyard falls six feet. As he stops, the harness and lanyard stretch 42 inches (or 3 and a half feet). What is the force on him and the rigging that supports him?

2. A 16-pound lighting instrument falls one foot. As it stops, the safety cable stretches one inch. What is the force on the instrument and rigging that supports it?

3. A 95-pound mover falls 18 inches. As it stops, the safety cable stretches one inch. What is the force on the instrument and rigging that supports it?

4. A 469- pound object falls 17 feet to the floor. The stopping distance is 4.6 feet. What is the shock load?

5. A 25- pound stage weight falls 75 feet to the deck. The stopping distance is 2.4 feet. What is the force on the object and the deck?

6. A 0.1- pound shackle pin falls 102 feet. It hits the deck with a stopping distance of 0.02 feet. What is the force on the pin when it hits the deck?

Answers

1. 543 lb

2. 216 lb

3. 1,876 lb

4. 2,202 lb

5. 806 lb

6. 505 lb

Shock load on wire rope

The equation for calculating the shock load when a wire rope "catches" a falling object is

$$Shock\ load = Load \times \left(1 + \sqrt{1 + \frac{2 \times Falling\ Distance \times Area \times Modulus\ of\ Elasticity}{Load \times Length \times 12}}\right)$$

where

Load is the weight of the falling object in pounds

Falling Distance is in inches

Length of wire rope is in feet

Modulus of Elasticity is in pounds per square inch (psi) – and is 15,000,000

Note: This is the Modulus of Elasticity for wire rope that had the structural stretch removed, either through pre-stretching or through use. New wire rope has a Modulus of Elasticity of 11,500,000 psi.

Area (Equivalent Metallic Area in square inches) = *Diameter of wire rope (in inches) × Diameter of wire rope (in inches) × Area Factor*

(See table below to find the area factor for the wire rope construction)

Construction of Wire Rope	Area Factor
7x7 GAC	0.471
7x19 GAC	0.472
6x19W with fiber core	0.416
6x19W with IWRC	0.482
6x36WS with fiber core	0.419
6x36WS with IWRC	0.485
8x19W with fiber core	0.366
8x19W with IWRC	0.497

So, a 200-pound object is connected to a 10-foot length of ¼" diameter 7x19 GAC, and free-falls 1 foot (12 inches). What is the shock load on the wire rope and the beam to which it is attached?

Area $= 0.25 \times 0.25 \times 0.472$

Area $= 0.0295$ square inches

$$\text{Shock load} = \text{Load} \times \left(1 + \sqrt{1 + \frac{2 \times \text{Falling Distance} \times \text{Area} \times \text{E}}{\text{Load} \times \text{Length} \times 12}} \right)$$

$$\text{Shock load} = \text{Load} \times \left(1 + \sqrt{1 + \frac{2 \times 12 \times 0.0295 \times 15,000,000}{200 \times 10 \times 12}} \right)$$

$$\text{Shock load} = \text{Load} \times \left(1 + \sqrt{1 + \frac{10,620,000}{24,000}} \right)$$

$$\text{Shock load} = \text{Load} \times \left(1 + \sqrt{1 + 442.5} \right)$$

$$\text{Shock load} = \text{Load} \times \left(1 + \sqrt{443.5} \right)$$

$$\text{Shock load} = \text{Load} \times \left(1 + 21.059 \right)$$

$$\text{Shock load} = 200 \times 21.059$$

Shock load $= 4,411.88$ lb

Problems

7. A 225-pound object is connected to a 95-foot length of 1/4" diameter 7x7 GAC, and free-falls 2 feet (24 inches). What is the shock load on the wire rope and the beam to which it is attached?

8. A 2,850-pound object is connected to a 110-foot length of 1/2" diameter 6x36WS with IWRC, and free-falls 7 feet (84 inches). What is the shock load on the wire rope and the beam to which it is attached?

9. A 3,900-pound object is connected to a 55-foot length of 3/4" diameter 6x36WS with fiber core, and free-falls 8 feet (96 inches). What is the shock load on the wire rope and the beam to which it is attached?

10. A 3,050-pound object is connected to a 36.8-foot length of 1/2" diameter 6x19W with fiber core, and free-falls 16 feet (192 inches). What is the shock load on the wire rope and the beam to which it is attached?

11. A 170-pound scenic flat is connected to a 22-foot length of 1/8" diameter 7x19 GAC, and free-falls 4 feet (48 inches). What is the shock load on the wire rope and the batten to which it is attached?

12. A 1,550-pound rigging point is connected to a 40-foot length of 3/8" diameter 7x19 GAC, and free-falls 3.5 feet (42 inches). What is the shock load on the wire rope and the rigging to which it is attached?

Answers

7. 2,283 lb

8. 28,692 lb

9. 67,352 lb

10. 67,445 lb

11. 2,791 lb

12. 18,057 lb

Shock loads on fiber rope

Different rope manufactures supply different data on the elasticity of their ropes and have different methods for calculating shock loads. We will look at the data provided by two rope companies, New England Ropes and Yale Cordage, and show how to calculate shock loads on each.

Method #1

$$Shock\ Load = \frac{-B + \sqrt{B^2 - (4 \times A \times C)}}{4 \times A}$$

where

A = (0.005 × Rope Stretch × Rope Length)/ Rope Load

B = -2 × A × Load

C = - Load × Fall Distance (in feet)

Rope stretch – rope stretch in percent as specified by the manufacturer. Put the number in as a percent – i.e. New England Ropes KMIII 7/16" rope stretches 5.1 percent, so put in "5.1" into the equation for calculating "A" above.

Note: You can find rope stretch (elongation) data for New England Ropes on pages 143 and 144 of Rigging Math Made Simple, Second Edition.

Rope length – the length of the rope, in feet, between the Load and the termination point.

Rope load – the force that the manufacturer specifies will causes the stretch specified, e.g. for New England Ropes KMIII, the rope stretches 5.1% at 10% of the minimum breaking strength (MBS). The MBS is 7083 pounds, so the rope load is .1 x 7083 pounds = 708 pounds.

Load – weight of object that falls

Fall – distance in feet that the Load free falls

Example: A 200-pound object is connected to a 10-foot length of 1/2" diameter Multiline II, and free-falls 1 foot. What is the shock load on the rope and the beam to which it is attached?

Multiline II has an elongation rate of 1.7% at 10% of its tensile strength. Since the tensile strength of ½" diameter Multiline II is 6,000 pounds, 10% would be 600 pounds.

$$A = \frac{0.005 \times 1.7 \times 10}{600}$$

$$A = 0.000141667$$

$$B = -2 \times 0.000141667 \times 200$$
$$B = -0.056666667$$

$$C = - \text{Load} \times \text{Fall Distance (in feet)}$$
$$C = - 200 \times 1$$
$$C = -200$$

Plugging these numbers into our equation, we get

$$\text{Shock Load} = \frac{-B + \sqrt{B^2 - (4 \times A \times C)}}{4 \times A}$$

$$\text{Shock Load} = \frac{0.056666667 + \sqrt{-0.0566666667^2 - (4 \times 0.000141667 \times -200)}}{4 \times 0.000141667}$$

$$\text{Shock Load} = \frac{0.056666667 + \sqrt{0.003211111 - (-0.1133336)}}{0.000566668}$$

$$\text{Shock Load} = \frac{0.056666667 + \sqrt{0.116544711}}{0.000566668}$$

$$\text{Shock Load} = \frac{0.056666667 + 0.341386454}{0.000566668}$$

$$\text{Shock Load} = \frac{0.398053254}{0.000566668}$$

Shock load = 702.45 lb

Problems

13. A 143- pound scenic load is connected to a 35-foot length of 3/16" diameter 3-Strand Spun Poly fiber rope manufactured by New England Ropes. The load free-falls 5 feet. What is the shock load on the fiber rope and the batten to which it is attached?

14. A 500- pound load is connected to a 50-foot length of 3/8" diameter Multiline II fiber rope manufactured by New England Ropes. The load free-falls 6.5 feet. What is the shock load on the fiber rope and the rigging to which it is attached?

15. An 1,840- pound load is connected to a 45-foot length of 3/8" diameter Sta-Set (white) fiber rope manufactured by New England Ropes. The load free-falls 4.4 feet. What is the shock load on the fiber rope and the rigging to which it is attached?

16. A 7,350- pound load is connected to a 85-foot length of 3/4" diameter Premium 3-Strand Nylon fiber rope manufactured by New England Ropes. The load free-falls 5.3 feet. What is the shock load on the fiber rope and the rigging to which it is attached?

17. A 5,300- pound load is connected to a 25-foot length of 5/8" diameter Multiline II fiber rope manufactured by New England Ropes. The load free-falls 9 feet. Using a 20% of elongation of Tensile Strength, what is the shock load on the fiber rope and the rigging to which it is attached?

Answers

13. 286 lb

14. 1,105 lb

15. 3,640 lb

16. 8,249 lb

17. 7,084 lb

Method #2

Yale Cordage does not list the elongation of their ropes in percentages of the breaking strength as New England Rope does, so the equation above will not work. Instead, Yale Cordage provides energy absorption data that is based on the weight of each rope. For example, Yale Cordage's Double Esterlon rope, a low stretch rope, has a "green working energy absorption" of 291 foot-pounds per pound of rope. A 5/8" Double Esterlon rope weights 13.7 pounds per 100 feet (or .137 pounds for foot) and has a recommended working load limit of 3,400 pounds at 20% of its breaking strength (a 5:1 design factor). As before, let's use a 200-pound load falling 1 foot on a 10-foot-long piece of rope.

First, we need to calculate the force of the fall:

Force = Load x Falling Distance
Force = 200 lb × 1 foot
Force = 200 foot lb

Next we calculate the energy absorption capacity of our rope using Yale Cordage's equation:

Energy Absorption Capacity = Length of Rope × Green Working Energy Absorption × Weight of 1 foot of rope

Energy Absorption Capacity = 10 feet × 291 foot pounds² × 0.137 pounds per foot
Energy Absorption Capacity = 398.67 foot pounds

Since the force being placed on the rope (200 foot pounds) is less than the Energy Absorption Capacity (398.67 foot pounds²) of the rope, we know that the rope will be able to sustain the shock load without failing. However, to find the actual shock load on the rope, we use the equation

$$Shock\ Load = \frac{Force}{Energy\ Absorbing\ Capacity} \times Recommended\ Working\ Load$$

So, for Yale's 5/8" diameter Double Esterlon rope (which has a working load limit of 3,400 pounds at 5:1):

$$Shock\ Load = \frac{200}{398.67} \times 3,400$$

Shock load = 1,705.67 lb

Problems

For Problems 18-22, use the following table:

Double Esterlon

Diameter	Working Load (lb)	Weight per 100 feet (lb)
1/2"	2,160	8.1
9/16"	2,740	9.6
5/8"	3,400	13.7
3/4"	4,160	16.3
7/8"	6,200	23.7
1"	8,800	35.2

Green working: 291 ft lb/lb
Red ultimate: 7,711 ft lb/lb

18. A 450- pound load is connected to a 25-foot length of Yale's Double Esterlon 5/8" diameter rope. The load free-falls 9 feet. Using the Yale Cordage Data Sheet:
    Calculate the force of the fall.
    Calculate the Energy Absorption Capacity
    What is the shock load on the fiber rope and the rigging to which it is attached?

19. 575- pound load is connected to a 90-foot length of Yale's Double Esterlon 5/8" diameter rope. The load free-falls 12 feet. Using the Yale Cordage Data Sheet:
    Calculate the force of the fall.
    Calculate the Energy Absorption Capacity
    What is the shock load on the fiber rope and the rigging to which it is attached?

20. A 1,000-pound load is connected to a 100-foot length of Yale's Double Esterlon 3/4" diameter rope. The load free-falls 8 feet. Using the Yale Cordage Data Sheet:
    Calculate the force of the fall.

Calculate the Energy Absorption Capacity

What is the shock load on the fiber rope and the rigging to which it is attached?

21. A 255- pound load is connected to a 60-foot length of Yale's Double Esterlon 3/8" diameter rope.

    The load free-falls 4 feet.

    Calculate the force of the fall.

    Calculate the Energy Absorption Capacity

    What is the shock load on the fiber rope and the rigging to which it is attached?

22. A 302- pound load is connected to a 95-foot length of Yale's Double Esterlon 1/2" diameter rope.

    The load free-falls 5 feet.

    Calculate the force of the fall.

    Calculate the Energy Absorption Capacity

    What is the shock load on the fiber rope and the rigging to which it is attached?

Answers

18. Force of Fall = 4,050 lb

    Energy Absorption Capacity = 997 foot pounds

    Shock load = 13,816 lb

19. Force of Fall = 6,900 lb

    Energy Absorption Capacity = 3,588.03 foot pounds

    Shock load = 6,538.40 lb

20. Force of Fall = 8,000 lb

    Energy Absorption Capacity = 4,743.3 foot pounds

    Shock load = 7,016.21 lb

21. Force of Fall = 1,020 lb

    Energy Absorption Capacity = 733.32 foot pounds

    Shock load= 1,557.84 lb

22. Force of Fall = 1,510 lb

    Energy Absorption Capacity = 2,239.24 foot pounds

    Shock load= 1,456.56 lb

Problems

For Problems 23-27, use the following table:

Yalex

Diameter	Working Load (lb)	Weight per 100 feet (lb)
1/4"	500	2.1
5/16"	800	2.8
3/8"	1,200	4
7/16"	1,800	7.1
1/2"	2,500	9
9/16"	3,300	11.2
5/8"	3,640	12.7
3/4"	4,800	17
7/8"	7,100	25.6
1"	8,600	32.3
1-1/8"	11,200	34.9
1-1/4"	13,100	39.3
1-5/16"	14,950	46.6
1-1/2"	18,700	60
1-5/8"	22,500	83
1-3/4"	24,000	94
2"	26,640	117

Green working: 409 ft lb/lb
Red ultimate: 10,700 ft lb/lb

23. A 205- pound load is connected to a 45-foot length of Yalex Single Braid 12- Strand 3/8" diameter rope. The load free-falls 7 feet.
    Calculate the force of the fall.
    Calculate the Energy Absorption Capacity
    What is the shock load on the fiber rope and the rigging to which it is attached?

24. A 438- pound load is connected to a 60-foot length of Yalex Single Braid 12- Strand 5/8" diameter rope. The load free-falls 14 feet.
    Calculate the force of the fall.
    Calculate the Energy Absorption Capacity
    What is the shock load on the fiber rope and the rigging to which it is attached?

25. A 322- pound load is connected to a 100-foot length of Yalex Single Braid 12- Strand 1/2" diameter rope. The load free-falls 6 feet. Using the Yale Cordage Data Sheet:
    Calculate the force of the fall.
    Calculate the Energy Absorption Capacity
    What is the shock load on the fiber rope and the rigging to which it is attached?

26. A 89- pound load is connected to a 23-foot length of Yalex Single Braid 12- Strand 3/8" diameter rope. The load free-falls 20 feet. Using the Yale Cordage Data Sheet:
    Calculate the force of the fall.
    Calculate the Energy Absorption Capacity
    What is the shock load on the fiber rope and the rigging to which it is attached?

27. A 204- pound load is connected to a 50-foot length of Yalex Single Braid 12- Strand 5/8" diameter rope. The load free-falls 45 feet. Using the Yale Cordage Data Sheet:
    Calculate the force of the fall.
    Calculate the Energy Absorption Capacity
    What is the shock load on the fiber rope and the rigging to which it is attached?

Answers

23. Force of Fall = 1,435 lb
    Energy Absorption Capacity = 736.2 foot pounds
    Shock load = 2,339.03 lb

24. Force of Fall = 6,132 lb
    Energy Absorption Capacity = 3,116.58 foot pounds
    Shock load= 7,161.85 lb

25. Force of Fall = 1,932 lb
    Energy Absorption Capacity = 3,681 foot pounds
    Shock load = 1,312.14 lb

26. Force of Fall = 1,780 lb
    Energy Absorption Capacity = 376.28 foot pounds
    Shock load = 5,676.62 lb

27. Force of Fall = 9,180 lb
    Energy Absorption Capacity = 2,597.15 foot pounds
    Shock load = 12,866.10 lb.

Problems

For Problems 28-32, use the following table:

Portland Braid

Diameter	Working Load (lb)	Weight per 100 feet (lb)
1/4"	460	2.2
5/16"	720	3.5
3/8"	980	5
7/16"	1,320	6.3
1/2"	1,680	8.8
9/16"	2,220	11.6
5/8"	2,980	14.1
3/4"	3,600	18
7/8"	5,890	27.1
1"	7,680	36.6
1-1/8"	9,00	43.5
1-1/4"	10,400	54
1-1/2"	13,400	69.2
1-3/4"	19,00	103
2"	23,600	127.4
2-1/2"	32,00	172.6

Green working: 265 ft lb/lb
Red ultimate: 5,929 ft lb/lb

28. A 160- pound load is connected to a 55-foot length of 3/8" diameter Portland Braid rope. The load free-falls 4.4 feet.

    Calculate the force of the fall.

    Calculate the Energy Absorption Capacity

    What is the shock load on the fiber rope and the rigging to which it is attached?

29. A 223- pound load is connected to a 65-foot length of 5/8" diameter Portland Braid rope. The load free-falls 6.5 feet.

    Calculate the force of the fall.

    Calculate the Energy Absorption Capacity

    What is the shock load on the fiber rope and the rigging to which it is attached?

30. A 1,010- pound load is connected to a 85-foot length of 3/4" diameter Portland Braid rope. The load free-falls 7.2 feet.
    Calculate the force of the fall.
    Calculate the Energy Absorption Capacity
    What is the shock load on the fiber rope and the rigging to which it is attached?

31. A 543- pound load is connected to a 110-foot length of 5/8" diameter Portland Braid rope. The load free-falls 3.6 feet.
    Calculate the force of the fall.
    Calculate the Energy Absorption Capacity
    What is the shock load on the fiber rope and the rigging to which it is attached?

32. A 865- pound load is connected to a 65-foot length of 1.5" diameter Portland Braid rope. The load free-falls 8.8 feet.
    Calculate the force of the fall.
    Calculate the Energy Absorption Capacity
    What is the shock load on the fiber rope and the rigging to which it is attached

Answers

28. Force of Fall = 704 lb
    Energy Absorption Capacity = 728.75 foot pounds
    Shock load = 946.71 lb

29. Force of Fall = 1,449.5 lb
    Energy Absorption Capacity = 2,428.72 foot pounds
    Shock load = 1,778.50 lb

30. Force of Fall = 7,272 lb
    Energy Absorption Capacity = 4,054.5 foot pounds
    Shock load= 6,456.82 lb

31. Force of Fall= 1,954.8 lb
    Energy Absorption Capacity = 4,110.15 foot pounds
    Shock load = 1,417.29 lb

32. Force of Fall = 7,612 lb
    Energy Absorption Capacity = 11,919.7 foot pounds
    Shock load = 8,557.32 lb

Chain Hoists and Shock Forces

A simple formula for quickly calculating an approximate shock force of a chain hoist stating and stopping is:

$$Shock\ Load = Load + \left(\frac{Speed\ of\ hoist\ in\ fpm}{60} \times Load\right)$$

So, if a 64-fpm chain hoist was used to lift a 1000-pound load, the approximate shock load would be:

$$Shock\ Load = 1000 + \left(\frac{64}{60} \times 1000\right)$$

$$Shock\ Load = 1000 + (1.0666667 \times 1000)$$

$$Shock\ Load = 1000 + 1066.67$$

$$\textbf{Shock Load} = \textbf{2,066.67 lb}$$

Problems

33. A 16-fpm chain hoist is used to lift a 1,800- pound load. What is the approximate shock load produced while starting and stopping?

34. A 16-fpm chain hoist is used to lift a 1,304- pound load. What is the approximate shock load produced while starting and stopping?

35. A 32-fpm chain hoist is used to lift a 1,932- pound load. What is the approximate shock load produced while starting and stopping?

36. A 16-fpm chain hoist is used to lift a 1,304- pound load. What is the approximate shock load produced while starting and stopping?

37. A 64-fpm chain hoist is used to lift a 1,577- pound load. What is the approximate shock load produced while starting and stopping?

38. A 64-fpm chain hoist is used to lift a 894- pound load. What is the approximate shock load produced while starting and stopping?

39. A 16-fpm chain hoist is used to lift a 3,400- pound load. What is the approximate shock load produced while starting and stopping?

40. A 32-fpm chain hoist is used to lift a 2,599- pound load. What is the approximate shock load produced while starting and stopping?

Answers

33. 2,280 lb

34. 1,651.73 lb

35. 2,962.4 lb

36. 1,651.73 lb

37. 3,259.13 lb

38. 1,847.6 lb

39. 4,306.66 lb

40. 3,985.13 lb

Chapter 26:
Wind and Water

Calculate Wind Loads

The calculate wind loads, follow the following steps:

Step 1. Calculate the force exerted by the wind on the structure by first squaring the wind speed (in miles per hour) and then multiplying the answer by 0.00256.

For a 30 mph wind the calculation would be

$$30 \times 30 \times 0.00256 = \textbf{2.304 lb per square foot}$$

Step 2. Multiply the force determined in Step 1 by the structure's surface area. With a 30 mph wind and a structure with a surface area of 100 square-feet, the calculation is

$$2.304 \times 100 = \textbf{230.4 lb}$$

Step 3. Multiply your answer from Step 2 by the structure's drag coefficient. For a flat square structure, multiply by 2.0. For a rounded structure, use 1.2.

For a flat structure with a surface area of 100 square feet, a 30 mph wind would create a wind load of

$$230.4 \times 2.0 = \textbf{460.8 lb}$$

Problems

1. What is the wind force on a flat, square 15' x 15' surface when the wind speed is 20 mph?

2. What is the wind force on a flat, square 23' x 35' surface when the wind speed is 45 mph?

3. What is the wind force on a flat, square 40' x 50' surface when the wind speed is 60 mph?

4. What is the wind force on a flat, square 25' x 43' surface when the wind speed is 10 mph?

5. What is the wind force on a rounded 45' x 55' surface when the wind speed is 43 mph?

6. What is the wind force on a rounded 5' x 15' surface when the wind speed is 50 mph?

7. What is the wind force on a flat, square 18' x 12' surface when the wind speed is 18 mph?

8. What is the wind force on a rounded 10.4' x 18.5' surface when the wind speed is 40 mph?

9. What is the wind force on a flat, squared 33.5' x 41' surface when the wind speed is 22 mph?

10. What is the wind force on a flat, squared 28' x 70' surface when the wind speed is 21 mph?

11. What is the wind force on a rounded 30' x 38.6' surface when the wind speed is 74 mph?

12. What is the wind force on a flat, squared 34' x 56.2' surface when the wind speed is 42 mph?

13. What is the wind force on a flat, squared 10' x 12.5' surface when the wind speed is 42 mph?

14. What is the wind force on a flat, squared 18.9' x 22.5' surface when the wind speed is 38 mph?

15. What is the wind force on a rounded 28' x 48' surface when the wind speed is 53 mph?

Answers

1. 460.8 pounds per square ft

2. 8,346.24 pounds per square ft

3. 36,864 pounds per square ft

4. 550.4 pounds per square ft

5. 14,058.31 pounds per square ft

6. 576 pounds per square ft

7. 358.31 pounds per square ft

8. 945.68 pounds per square ft

9. 3,403.64 pounds per square ft

10. 4,425.52 pounds per square ft

11. 19,480.19 pounds per square ft

12. 17,257.73 pounds per square ft

13. 1,128.96 pounds per square ft

14. 3143.99 pounds per square ft

15. 11597.70 pounds per square ft

Weight of Water

A one-inch deep pool of water weights 5.202 pounds per square foot (or 62.428 pounds per cubic foot). So, Use the following formula to calculate the weight of the water:

Weight = Depth of water x 5.202 × area (width of pool × length of pool)

Example: The weight of one inch of standing water on a 100' x 100' surface (such as a roof) would be:

Weight = 1 x 5.202 × 100 × 100
Weight = 52,020 pounds

Problems

16. What is the weight of a pool of water 10' x 18' that is 2 inches deep?

17. What is the weight of a pool of water 50' x 50' that is 1 inch deep?

18. What is the weight of a pool of water 18.6' x 33.6' that is 4 inches deep?

19. What is the weight of a pool of water 23' x 55' that is 3 inches deep?

20. What is the weight of a pool of water 42.7' x 54.2' that is 6 inches deep?

21. What is the weight of a pool of water 35.4' x 40.8' that is 5 inches deep?

Answers

16. 1873 lb

17. 13,005 lb

18. 13004 lb

19. 19,7429 lb

20. 72,236 lb

21. 7,567 lb

Weight of Ice

Weight of ice = Thickness of ice × 0.92 x 5.202 × area

Problems

22. What is the weight of a sheet of ice 100' x 100' that is 1 inch deep?

23. What is the weight of a sheet of ice 45' x 45' that is 2 inches deep?

24. What is the weight of a sheet of ice 24' x 27' that is 2 inches deep?

25. What is the weight of a sheet of ice 29' x 53.6' that is 1 inch deep?

26. What is the weight of a sheet of ice 40.4' x 83.2' that is 5 inches deep?

27. A roof structure has a pool of water measuring 45' x 48' x 2". On top of the pool is a sheet of ice measuring 40' x 43' x 1". Calculate the total weight of the water and the ice on the structure.

28. A roof structure has a pool of water measuring 32' x 54' x 3". On top of the pool is a sheet of ice measuring 30' x 52' x 1". Calculate the total weight of the water and the ice on the structure.

29. A roof structure has a pool of water measuring 28' x 17' x 2". On top of the pool is a sheet of ice measuring 15' x 13' x 1". Calculate the total weight of the water and the ice on the structure.

Answers

22. 47,858 lb

23. 19,383 lb

24. 6,202 lb

25. 7,439 lb

26. 80,433 lb

27. Water = 22,473 lb, Ice = 8,323 lb, Total = 30,705 lb

28. Water = 26,967 lb, Ice = 7,466 lb, Total = 34,4329 lb

29. Water = 4,952 lb, Ice = 933 lb, Total = 5,885 lb

Weight of Snow

Weight of snow = Depth of snow on surface × percentage of water × area × 5.2

So, if the snow is 1 foot deep and the percentage of water is 10 percent, and the area is 100' x 100', the weight of the snow is:

Weight of snow $= 12 \times 0.10 \times 10,000 \times 5.2$
Weight of snow $= 1.2 \times 10,000 \times 5.2$
Weight of snow $= 1.2 \times 52,000$
Weight of snow = 62,400 lb or 6.24 lb per square foot

Problems

30. If the snow on a roof is 16 inches deep, the percentage of water is 20 percent, and the area is 50' x 50', calculate the weight of the snow on the structure.

31. If the snow on a roof is 18 inches deep, the percentage of water is 30 percent, and the area is 25' x 30', calculate the weight of the snow on the structure.

32. If the snow on a roof is 24 inches deep, the percentage of water is 17 percent, and the area is 20' x 25', calculate the weight of the snow on the structure.

33. If the snow on a roof is 8 inches deep, the percentage of water is 50 percent, and the area is 30' x 45', calculate the weight of the snow on the structure.

34. If the snow on a roof is 3 inches deep, the percentage of water is 6 percent, and the area is 15' x 18', calculate the weight of the snow on the structure.

35. If the snow on a roof is 11 inches deep, the percentage of water is 22 percent, and the area is 18' x 33', calculate the weight of the snow on the structure.

36. If the snow on a roof is 22 inches deep, the percentage of water is 13 percent, and the area is 50' x 50', calculate the weight of the snow on the structure.

Answers

30. 41,600 lb

31. 21,060 lb

32. 10,698 lb

33. 28,080 lb

34. 252.72 lb

35. 7,474.89 lb

36. 37,180 lb

Chapter 27:

Motor Calculations

Example: What horsepower motor is needed to lift a 250 lb load at 30 feet per minute (.5 feet per second) with an acceleration time of 1.5 seconds?

The first step is to calculate the Adjusted weight. The formula to do this is:

Adjusted weight = (Load / 32.2) × (32.2 + (Speed in fps / Acceleration time))

So, plugging in the numbers from the problem we get:

Adjusted weight = (250 / 32.2) × (32.2 + (.5 / 1.5))

Adjusted weight = (7.763975155 × (32.2 + 0.333))

Adjusted weight = 7.763975155 × 32.533

Adjusted weight = 252.59 lb

To calculate the Horsepower of the motor, use the formula:

Horsepower = (Speed *Adjusted weight) / 550

So ...

Horsepower = (.5 x 252.59) / 550

Horsepower = 126.295)/ 550

Horsepower = 0.23

Problems

1. What horsepower motor is needed to lift a 300 lb load at 60 feet per minute with an acceleration time of 2.5 seconds?

2. What horsepower motor is needed to lift a 1,000 lb load at 8 feet per second with an acceleration time of 3 seconds?

3. What horsepower motor is needed to lift a 400 lb load at 12 feet per second with an acceleration time of 0.6 seconds?

4. What horsepower motor is needed to lift an 1,800 lb load at 16 feet per minute with an acceleration time of .5 seconds?

5. What horsepower motor is needed to lift a 2,000 lb load at 32 feet per minute with an acceleration time of 0.5 seconds?

6. What horsepower motor is needed to lift a 1,500 lb load at 64 feet per minute with an acceleration time of 2 seconds?

7. What horsepower motor is needed to lift a 150 lb actor at 8 feet per second with an acceleration time of 1 second?

8. What horsepower motor is needed to lift a load of 348 lb on a scenic elevator at 8 feet per second with an acceleration time of 4 seconds?

9. What horsepower motor is needed to lift a load of 1,005 lb at 25 feet per minute with an acceleration time of 3 seconds?

10. What horsepower motor is needed to lift a 2,500 lb load at 25 feet per minute with an acceleration time of 0.75 seconds?

11. What horsepower motor is needed to lift a 469 lb load at 18.5 feet per minute with an acceleration time of 5 seconds?

12. What horsepower motor is needed to lift a 925 lb load at 0.45 feet per second with an acceleration time of 3 seconds?

13. What horsepower motor is needed to lift a 3,890 lb load at 4 feet per second with an acceleration time of 4 seconds?

14. What horsepower motor is needed to lift a 4,392 lb load at 19 feet per minute with an acceleration time of 7 seconds?

15. What horsepower motor is needed to lift a 1-ton load at 27 feet per minute with an acceleration time of 2 seconds?

16. What horsepower motor is needed to lift a ½-ton load at 55 feet per minute with an acceleration time of 6.5 seconds?

17. What horsepower motor is needed to lift a 1,953 lb load at 2.9 feet per second with an acceleration time of 0.6 seconds?

18. What horsepower motor is needed to lift a 4,390 lb load at 48 feet per minute with an acceleration time of 3.5 seconds?

19. What horsepower motor is needed to lift a 1/4-ton load at 18 feet per second with an acceleration time of 0.28 seconds?

20. What horsepower motor is needed to lift a 641 lb load at 100 feet per minute with an acceleration time of 10.5 seconds?

Answers

1. 0.55 horsepower

2. 15.75 horsepower

3. 14.15 horsepower

4. 0.89 horsepower

5. 2.00 horsepower

6. 2.96 horsepower

7. 2.72 horsepower

8. 5.38 horsepower

9. 0.77 horsepower

10. 1.92 horsepower

11. 0.26 horsepower

12. 0.76 horsepower

13. 29.17 horsepower

14. 2.53 horsepower

15. 1.65 horsepower

16. 1.67 horsepower

17. 11.83 horsepower

18. 6.65 horsepower

19. 49.03 horsepower

20. 1.95 horsepower

38659210R10121

Made in the USA
San Bernardino, CA
10 September 2016